Hebrews
THE GLORIOUS JESUS

MIKE MAZZALONGO

Line by Line Bible Studies

Line by line, verse by verse. These studies are designed to bring out the simple meaning of the biblical text for the modern reader.

ISBN: 978-0-69266-984-6

BibleTalk Books
14998 E. Reno
Choctaw, Oklahoma 73020

TABLE OF CONTENTS

CHAPTER 1
INTRODUCTION

Hebrews 1:1-3

The first Christians were Jewish. The first congregation of the Lord's church was made up of Jewish people. The first Scriptures used to prove Christ as the Messiah were the Jewish Scriptures which we refer to as the Old Testament. It took approximately ten years for the Apostles to preach the gospel to non-Jews (Cornelius and his household - Acts 10). In the first 30 years of Christianity you could be a Hebrew Christian and still practice your Jewish faith and traditions because the two religions were seen as different forms of the same thing. Eventually, however, this became more difficult for a variety of reasons:

- The Jewish religion became more hostile towards Christianity (Saul's persecution, Acts 9:1ff).

- Conservative Jewish Christians wanted to keep Christianity within the context and control of the Jewish religion (Judaizers, Acts 9:1ff).

- The Roman government began making a distinction between the two religions (they had seen Christianity as a sect within Judaism). Only Judaism was a lawful religion within the Roman Empire, so Christianity along with other religions were banned by the government (Paul's execution, II Timothy 4:6).

Because of these pressures, many Jewish Christians were faced with the decision to either return to their former religion or make a complete break with Judaism in order to fully embrace Christianity. They could no longer have it both ways. The letter to the Hebrews, therefore, was written to convince them that in becoming Christians they had made the right choice and they were to persevere in that choice (Hebrews 6:11).

Title

The full title of this epistle is, "To the Hebrews." It was not written as a general epistle to all Jews, but it could have been used in this way if necessary. This letter, therefore, was addressed to a specific group that the author knew and was planning to visit (Hebrews 13:23).

Authorship

There is no definitive proof but there are several theories as to who wrote this epistle:

- An unknown writer who knew Paul's writings and wrote this letter using these as source material.

- **Barnabas** - He was a Levite (Acts 4:36), so was familiar with Jewish ritual and Old Testament customs. He wrote Greek since he came from Cyprus. He was not known for his scholarity but rather as a man of action, and yet this epistle was written using an educated form of the Greek language.

- **Apollos** - He was a Greek scholar and orator from Alexandria, well versed in the Old Testament as well as Paul's writings. He was well known and respected in the church, however none of his other writings exist and he doesn't name himself in the text.

- **Paul** - This Apostle was familiar with the Old Testament and the Gospel. He may have first written it as a sermon (many references suggest an oral presentation, Hebrews 1:1). All early church fathers (Clement 156 AD-211 AD; Origin 185 AD-254 AD; Jerome 347 AD-420 AD) concluded that it was written by Paul. The best guess or theory is that it was originally written by Paul as a sermon, and later translated into Greek by Luke during or after Paul's death in Rome (67 AD).

What we know for sure is that the writer knew his readers and their circumstances; knew Timothy; was well versed in the Old Testament and temple ritual; fully grasped the knowledge of who Christ was; and was an excellent writer. But as Origen said after his study of the question, "But who wrote the epistle only God knows certainly."

Date

- **96 AD** - Clement, Bishop of Rome, quotes from Hebrews so it's definitely before 96 AD.

- **70 AD** - The city of Jerusalem and the Temple are destroyed by the Roman army. Since the book of Hebrews deals with temple ritual at length, the fact that this event is not mentioned in the epistle strongly suggests that it was written before 70 AD. Also, the work of the priests is referred to in present tense.

- **33-60 AD** - Hebrews 2:3-4; 13:7 speak of leaders in the church and those who have given leadership examples, and have since passed on. This suggests that at least a generation or two have taken place since the initial establishment of the church in Jerusalem.

Most scholars put the writing between 63-69 AD because the temple is still standing and functioning, and there has been time for several generations of Christian leaders to have been raised up in the church.

Purpose and Approach of Hebrews

> But I urge you brethren, bear with this word of exhortation, for I have written to you briefly.
> - Hebrews 13:22

The purpose of this epistle was to encourage Jewish Christians who were wavering in their faith and contemplating a return to Judaism to remain faithful to Christ.

- They were discouraged by persecution and being forced to choose.

- They began to neglect the assembly, which is usually a first sign of spiritual illness.

- Many had already returned to Judaism (Hebrews 6:4-6).

- It was becoming clear that the Jewish nation was not going to embrace Christianity.

- Jewish Christians were going to be isolated (didn't fit with Gentiles, rejected by their Jewish families).

Approach

The writer compares the two religions and challenges his readers to choose, once and for all, which is superior. In the epistle he compares Christ to various important features of the Jewish religion: the prophets, the angels, Moses, Joshua and Aaron, all who represented in one way or another the Jewish religion and its worship. Once he finishes his series of comparisons and arguments, the author lists a number of heroes who were persecuted and suffered for their faith, but persevered; this done as an encouragement for them to emulate. He completes the epistle with practical teaching about how to live faithfully from day to day as a Christian, and then finishes with greetings and exhortations.

General Outline

Hebrews is divided into two major parts:

1. **The Glory of Christ (Hebrews 1:1-10:18)**

   o The Jewish people were used to the concept that God revealed Himself through various ways, people, angels and religious rites (temple worship, sacrificial system). God glorified Himself and His people through these ways, and the people took confidence in and gave praise to God for this interaction throughout their history. In this first part of Hebrews the writer demonstrates that no matter how glorious these things were, the revelation (uncovering) we receive from God through Jesus Christ is far superior. Therefore, in the first ten chapters the writer demonstrates how Jesus is more glorious than prophets, angels, Moses, etc. and thus superior and worthy to be followed and obeyed.

2. **The Glory of the Church (Hebrews 10:19-13:25)**

- o Once he has established the supremacy of Christ by demonstrating His greater glory, the author encourages the church to glorify its head, Jesus, by faithfulness to Him and holiness in Him. The conclusion, left unsaid, is that if Jesus is more glorious than the Jewish religion (including its prophets, rituals, etc.), then His church shares that glory and is therefore superior also. (The argument being: don't abandon the greater for the lesser.)

Jesus: Greater than the Prophets - Hebrews 1:1-3

> [1] God, after He spoke long ago to the fathers in the prophets in many portions and in many ways,

"God spoke" - He was speaking, it was a personal and a conscious communication. "Fathers" were the various people, leaders, kings to whom God spoke throughout the history of Jewish people. "In the prophets" - God was speaking when they spoke. They (meaning the contents of the Old Testament) were the greatest single source of revelation. "Portions and ways" - Spoke through them in different ways: dreams, visions, writings - they sometimes gave immediate warnings, other times far off prophecy, and they performed miracles to authenticate their divine inspiration.

> [2a] in these last days has spoken to us in His Son

"These last days" refers to the last phase of human history according to biblical chronology. There are three historical phases:

1. **Antedeluvian** - From the creation to the flood (Genesis 1:1-8:22).

2. **Postdeluvian** - From the first rainbow after the flood to the ascension of Jesus (Genesis 9:1-Acts 1:26). Both begin and end with men's eyes looking toward the sky in hope.

3. **Last days** - Pentecost Sunday to the Second Coming of Jesus (Acts 2:1-Revelation 22:21). The time that the church has been given to prepare the world for the return of Christ. In this "last time" God has spoken through His Son, not the prophets or in other "various ways." This is the communication method from God in the last times. The revelation that He makes through His Son in these last times is greater than anything that had ever come from the prophets. Therefore, Jesus is greater than the prophets. Note that the writer isn't saying that God didn't speak through the prophets, He did, but Jesus was the person that they were speaking about. The writer goes on to list three things about the Son that demonstrates His superiority over the prophets.

1. His Pre-eminence in History

> [2] in these last days has spoken to us in His Son, whom He appointed heir of all things, through whom also He made the world.

An heir is one who inherits something left to him by someone else; usually the thing left has been gathered or built by one person and left to another to inherit. The writer here notes that Jesus is the inheritor of all things because through Him all things were created. This is not a new idea in the New Testament. Many passages refer to this idea of Christ's exalted position (Matthew 28:18, John 11:3, I Corinthians 8:6, Colossians 1:16-17, Revelation 1:8; "I Am the Alpha and Omega").

Jesus has a preeminent place in history because He is both at the beginning of history as the agent of creation, and at the end of creation as its inheritor (the rightful owner in place of Satan who tried to displace Him by seducing mankind). The prophets reminded the Jews of their past and spoke of the future, but Jesus is greater than they because He is at both the beginning and end of time, and the prophets lived only in between the beginning and the end of time.

2. His Person

> [3a] And He is the radiance of His glory and the exact representation of His nature, and upholds all things by the word of His power.

In discussing the personhood of Jesus, the author says three things about Jesus which no one could ever say about any of the prophets.

He is the "radiance of His glory." Radiance = light or brightness. Glory = source/essence of God. Jesus is light from the source, not reflected light (like the moon). He is like "sunlight." Moses' face shone as the radiance of God reflected off of him. Jesus' radiance in relationship to God is what flames are to fire, what sunlight is to the sun. We see this radiance in practical ways in His teaching, miracles, pure life; we see it in supernatural ways: His transfiguration and ascension. The prophets saw and spoke of this radiance, but Jesus was the radiance. Without Jesus the world is in complete darkness when it comes to God and salvation ("I am the light of the world" John 8:12).

He is the "exact representation of His nature." Some translations say "stamp" or "imprint" of God's nature. The idea here is that Jesus isn't a copy of God, He has the same nature as God. The clearest example of this "different but the same" idea is seen in the difference between male and female. Men and women are different in gender but have the same nature. In the same way, when we see Jesus, we see a person separate from God the Father, but one that has the same nature as God. The prophets did supernatural things by the power of God, but they only possessed a human nature. Jesus did supernatural things because He had both a human and a divine nature.

"He upholds all things by the word of His power." Upholds here doesn't mean "carrying" like the picture of Atlas holding the world on his shoulders. It means that His power holds everything together so that nothing is allowed to totally destroy the world.

He also guides the world to its end according to His purpose, and He cannot be overtaken in this. All of this is done by the power of His word or His expressed will uttered. For example, in the beginning God expressed His will by saying, "...let there be light" and light appeared. Converting God's expressed word into reality was Christ's role in creation. When in the boat during the storm, Jesus calmed the sea simply by expressing His will through His word (the power to convert His expressed will into object reality), and the stormy sea became a calm sea.

To the crippled man in the temple He offered forgiveness with just His word and then to prove that He had power even over unseen things like forgiveness of sins, He healed him, again with just His word. The prophets did many great things, but the words they spoke were His words and the things they did were done through His will. Jesus was greater than the prophets because He was before them and after them; His personhood reflected God's image, will and power; and finally, His position was greater than theirs.

3. His Position

> ^{3b} When He had made purification of sins, He sat down at the right hand of the Majesty on high,

The author describes the two positions that Jesus took that no prophet ever could.

1. As sacrifice for sin - the lowest position.

Jesus could have expressed His preeminence and personhood without leaving heaven, but He did so in order to deal with man's sin.

> who, although He existed in the form of God, did not regard equality with God a thing to be grasped, but emptied Himself, taking the form of a bond-servant, and being made in the likeness of men. Being found in appearance as a man, He humbled Himself by becoming obedient to the point of death, even death on a cross.
> - Philippians 2:6-8

This reference to purification from sin is explained further on as the author goes into more detail about the manner and reasons why this had to be done. Here he merely mentions that Jesus did it.

2. Right hand of God - the highest position (authority).

Philippians 2:8 explains that Jesus returned to reclaim the position of authority He occupied before His humiliation on the cross. It is interesting to note that Jesus is first and last in a horizontal time frame, and occupies the top and bottom roles in the vertical positions of honor, the top being His throne in heaven and the bottom being the cross He suffered. So horizontally He is at the beginning and at the end, and vertically He is at the top and the bottom as well.

The prophets offered sacrifices for sin, but never offered themselves as sacrifice. None of the prophets had authority save what they received from God. Most tried to run from God. Jesus, however, gives authority from His position of power at the right hand of God.

Summary

The author begins his letter by exalting Jesus. He says that He is greater than the prophets because:

- He is first and last in history - prophets lived in between history.
- He is divine in nature - prophets are only human.
- He is supreme in authority - prophets have no authority.

No prophet could or ever did claim such things.

Application

There's really only one main lesson or application based on our study of the first three verses of Hebrews chapter one: listen to Jesus Christ! At the transfiguration the voice in the cloud said,

> this is my beloved Son, with whom I am well pleased; listen to Him!
> - Matthew 17:5b

He is greater than the prophets of Israel, and they were greater than any of the prophets of their day or ours because what they said came true. Jesus, by His position historically (first and last) and spiritually (lowest and highest) has the right and authority to speak as and for God. When our faith is weak, when we are searching for answers, when we are troubled or discouraged, what we need is not more time alone, a vacation or a break from church; we need to listen to Jesus Christ!

To a church on the brink of collapse, the author, without introduction or preamble, gives them the life sustaining words about the glorious Jesus Christ. We should remember this when we find ourselves in this position or are trying to encourage others to persevere in their faith.

CHAPTER 2
JESUS: GREATER THAN THE ANGELS
PART 1

Hebrews 1:4-14

The book of Hebrews was written to a particular group of Jewish Christians who, because of persecution, were being tempted to abandon Christianity and return to Judaism. In his letter, the author appeals to them to remain faithful to Christ by showing them Christ's superiority to their former Jewish religion. He does this by comparing Jesus to various elements of the Jewish religion (prophets, angels, Moses, priesthood). In the previous chapter we studied how Jesus was superior to the prophets because:

- He was preeminent in history (first and last)
- He was divine in nature
- He was superior in position (authority)
  - at right hand of God

In this chapter we will see the author move from a comparison of Jesus and the prophets to a comparison of Jesus and the angels. Before we examine the comparison however, let's get a little background on angels themselves.

Angels

Both the Hebrew and Greek words for angel mean "messenger" or messenger from God. The word "angel" in the Bible refers to an order of spiritual/supernatural (not divine) created beings who act as God's messengers to men, and agents who carry out God's will among men.

- They are spirit beings and appear in the Bible as men (Genesis 18:2), but never as women or babies; created by God (Psalm 148:1-5; Colossians 1:16).

- They are not human and have no sensual desires (Matthew 12:25).

- Sometimes described as having wings (Isaiah 6:2; Daniel 9:21).

- They have intelligence and free will which explains why some (Satan) are condemned because of rebellion (II Peter 2:4).

- They were present and rejoiced at the creation of the world (Job 38:4-7) which suggests that they were created and rebelled before the creation of the world.

There are no personal descriptions of angels, only a description of their order and function:

- Heavenly powers - Psalm 29:1
- Holy ones - Psalm 89:5
- Watchers - Daniel 4:13

- Council (archangels) - Psalm 89:7
- Congregation (host) - Psalm 82:1
- Spirits - Hebrews 1:14
- Powers/princes/dominion (positive sense) - Colossians 1:16
- Powers/princes/dominion (negative sense) - Ephesians 6:12
- Archangels - I Thessalonians 4:16
- Angel of God/Lord (special "type" for Christ where terms angel and Lord are interchangeable) - Genesis 22:11-15
- Sons of God - Job 38:7

Angels serve God in a variety of ways:

- Messengers - Abraham (Genesis 19:13), Mary (Luke 1)
- Destroyers - Passover (Exodus 12)
- Ministers - desert (Matthew 4:11), garden (Luke 22:43)
- Worshippers - constantly praising God (Psalm 103:21)
- Guardians - God's people (Daniel 12:1), children (Psalm 103:1)

The Jews were familiar with the existence and appearance of these supernatural beings throughout their history. The prophets spoke God's words and did mighty miracles by God's power, but angels were super-human beings who were at God's throne and had appeared to them in person. For the Jews, angels represented one of their most powerful experiences of the supernatural.

Why the comparison between Jesus and angels?

Many Christians in the first century were confused as to how they should relate to Jesus (man only or God only). Some, especially Jewish Christians, may have been tempted to see Him as part of the angelic creation. After all, they were often sent by God as messengers and did mighty deeds. The author of Hebrews firmly establishes the identity of Jesus as being greater than angels. He also shows how Old Testament passages are fulfilled in Jesus Christ, and how these passages point to Jesus' superiority over the angels.

> having become as much better than the angels, as He has inherited a more excellent name than they.
> - Hebrews 1:4

He begins in verse 4 by making a summary statement concerning Jesus and angels.

1. He is much better than angels.

2. He has inherited a better "name" than they had. As a man Jesus was lower than the angels because He was confined to time and space. With His death, resurrection and ascension, however, He inherits a better name (position) than they have. He "inherits" because the position was rightfully His (He created everything so He deserves a better position). It is a better position because it is at the right hand of power, not the angelic "position" of service.

The author supports this claim with Scripture about the character and position of the Messiah in relationship to angels. This position was determined long before by God and spoken of by the prophets. He proves his point by referring to seven specific Old Testament passages that demonstrate the superiority of the Messiah in comparison to angels:

> For to which of the angels did He ever say,
> "You are My Son,
> Today I have begotten You"?
> - Hebrews 4:5a

This passage comes from Psalm 2 and refers to the enthronement of a king from David's line. On ascending the throne, the idea is that the king becomes God's son. The Scripture ultimately referred to the Messiah who would come from David's line and would rule forever (II Samuel 7:14-16). The point is that God calls the angels as a group "sons of God" (Job 1:6), but no one angel was ever referred to as the Son of God, like the Messiah was called. The term "begotten" refers to an enthronement - Jesus sits at the right hand of authority. So the author begins by showing that Jesus, the Messiah, is greater than angels because the prophets said that He would be called the Son of God, not a son, not sons of God like angles were called. He is greater because He is the Son of God.

> And again,
> "I will be a Father to Him
> And He shall be a Son to Me"?
> - Hebrew 4:5b

This passage comes from II Samuel 7:14 and refers to the promise that God made to David through Nathan the prophet, that God would provide for his son's efforts at building a temple in Jerusalem. The point here is that the Messiah (David's descendant through Solomon) would be like earthly kings; He would be a son, but unlike earthly kings, He would rule from heaven. He repeats the point that no angel was ever promised a thing like this by God, but the Messiah was, and Jesus is the Messiah.

> I also shall make him My first-born,
> the highest of the kings of the earth.
> - Psalm 89:27

Here the writer is not arguing that Jesus is the Messiah (his readers accept this), he is proposing that Jesus, as the Messiah, is greater than the angels according to Scripture.

> And when He again brings the firstborn into the world, He says,
> "And let all the angels of God worship Him."
> - Hebrews 1:6

This is a difficult verse because it could refer to the time when Jesus returns to the world, as in His second coming, the angels will worship Him then. The term "first-born" denotes priority and superiority over all those born, and not the first one created. For example, in the case of Esau and Jacob, Esau was the first one born but Jacob was "firstborn" as to position.

This quote from Psalm 97:7 is an exhortation that every person and every spiritual being must worship Divinity. The author uses the quotation to say that when Jesus was revealed as the Divine Son of God, even the angels should have worshiped Him as the Scripture says they should of Divinity. Jesus is not only greater than the angels but also deserving of worship from them. The "again" is usually seen as a literary device to introduce a new idea and should be at the beginning of the sentence.

> And of the angels He says,
> "Who makes His angels winds,
> And His ministers a flame of fire."
> - Hebrew 1:7

This is the Old Testament idea (Psalm 104:4) that God used His angels as His ministers; they were winds and flames in His service. The point is that angels have no authority, and at their highest they are servants. Supernatural beings but servants none the less. They do not give orders, they take them. In the next verses he compares the authority of Christ to that of the angels.

> [8] But of the Son He says,
> "Your throne, O God, is forever and ever,
> [9] And the righteous scepter is the scepter of His kingdom.
> "You have loved righteousness and hated lawlessness;
> Therefore God, Your God, has anointed You
> With the oil of gladness above Your companions."
> Hebrews 1:8-9

This passage is taken from Psalm 45:6-7 and in it the author describes the regal splendor of the position of king. As Messiah, Jesus rules as king in heaven. Unlike earthly kings however, Jesus rules:

- eternally (forever and ever)
- with authority (scepter of His kingdom)
- with justice (righteous, hated lawlessness)
- with joy (anointed with oil of gladness)

"Above Your companions" refers to the angels over whom He

rules. The angels in Old Testament literature stood before the throne of God, now the author pictures Jesus sitting on that throne.

> [10] And,
> "You, Lord, in the beginning laid the foundation of the earth,
> And the heavens are the works of Your hands;
> [11] They will perish, but You remain;
> And they all will become old like a garment,
> [12] And like a mantle You will roll them up;
> Like a garment they will also be changed.
> But You are the same,
> And Your years will not come to an end."
> - Hebrews 1:10-12

Psalm 102:25-27 reviews the Old Testament description of the Son as the creator, all powerful, eternal and preeminent (first and last). The point here is that angels are not creators because they have no creative power. They are created beings and are thus inferior to the Son. In the previous verses the author showed Jesus on the throne of the kingdom in heaven, here he demonstrates that His rule extends over the physical creation as well.

> [13] But to which of the angels has He ever said,
> "Sit at My right hand,
> Until I make Your enemies
> A footstool for Your feet"?
> [14] Are they not all ministering spirits, sent out to render service for the sake of those who will inherit salvation?
> - Hebrews 1:13-14

In Psalm 110:1 the author closes the argument concerning Christ and angels with an emphatic statement, "To what angel did God ever say..." The picture described here is that of the ancient custom of the victor putting his foot on the neck of a defeated enemy (Joshua 10:24). Only to His Son Jesus, the Messiah, does God offer the position of authority on the throne. This position Jesus takes as all of His enemies will finally bow to Him at the end of time (Philippians 2:10-11). But angels are servants of the Son towards the saints on earth. A final image of contrast between the son who has accomplished salvation and has returned to heaven to rule, and angels who minister to the saved on behalf of the Son.

Summary

The author uses Old Testament scriptures to demonstrate that, as the Messiah, Jesus is greater than the greatest of the supernatural creatures that they have ever known: angels.

1. He is greater because He is a Son of Divine origin and they are created sons.

2. He is greater because He is the fulfillment of God's plan according to promise and they have no such promise.

3. He is greater because as a divine being He is deserving of worship, and they offer worship.

4. He is greater because He has authority to command and they have only the free will to obey or disobey.

5. He is greater because He sits as king and they are merely servants of the king.

6. He is greater because He created the world and they are created beings.

7. He is greater because He saved men from sin and they only minister to saved mankind.

In this section the author establishes from Scripture Christ's higher position than the angels. In the second part of this section he will describe the significance of the work that Jesus did when, for a time, He accepted to be in a lower position than the angels.

Application

1. It's not how big your church is - it's how big your God is!

Mormons and Jehovah Witnesses deny the Bible's description of Jesus. Mormons teach that Jesus is one of many "sons" who became God, a kind of preexisting spirit. Jehovah Witnesses teach that Jesus began His existence as Michael the Archangel. And with these teachings they have built enormous followings with thousands of churches all over the world. Their advertising is slick, their zeal to spread their doctrines is powerful; but don't be fooled by the size of their churches, their wealth or their influence in the world. Their God is no god, their Jesus is not the Lord. The Jesus that the Hebrew writer describes: He is the Lord, He is the Savior. Don't judge the value of a person's religion by size or noise, ask them who their Lord is. If He's not the Lord of the angels, He's not our Lord.

2. Jesus is always more, not less.

From the very beginning there has always been an attempt to lessen who Jesus is:

1. "Is this not the carpenter's son...?" (Mark 6:3). The people in His home town hearing of His miracles and listening to His teaching remarked that He was just one of them - the lowly son of a carpenter.

2. "Do we not say rightly that you are a Samaritan and have a demon?" (John 8:48). The leaders accused Him of being less than a good Jew and demon possessed.

3. The people the Hebrew writer was addressing were tempted to see Him as part of the angelic beings they had known.

4. Various religions of the past and present have referred to Him as one of their own gods (Hinduism) or a great prophet (Muslims).

5. Modern philosophers view Him as a moral teacher and leader.

But any description of Him that brings Him down (even if it's done politely and respectfully) from His exalted position is inaccurate. John says "For many deceivers have gone out into the world, those who do not acknowledge Jesus Christ as coming in the flesh. This is the deceiver and the anti-Christ," (II John 7). John warns that the main deception will always be to deny the equally divine/human nature of Jesus. The Apostles taught that Jesus was God and nothing less than this (John 20:28). Any teaching or suggestion that is different than this is not biblical. John even says that teaching of this nature is part of the power of the anti-Christ in the world then and today. Jesus is always more than what we think or imagine - not less!

CHAPTER 3
JESUS: GREATER THAN THE ANGELS
PART 2

Hebrews 2

The book of Hebrews was written to first century Christian Jews who were contemplating returning to Judaism because of the persecution they were facing. The author encourages them to be faithful by demonstrating that Jesus Christ was superior to every element of their former Jewish religion. He begins by showing how Jesus is superior in position and nature to the prophets. Then he goes on to demonstrate that according to Old Testament prophecy, Jesus the Messiah was considered greater than the angels. This was an important point for the Jews since angels represented a significant part of their contact with supernatural beings, and they may have been tempted to consider Jesus as an angelic being and not a divine one. Once the author describes Jesus' rightful place at the right hand of God, far above the position of the angels, he warns his readers about the significance of this. He then explains the reasons why this exalted Jesus took, for a while at least, a position lower than the angels. This was another idea difficult for Jews to accept.

Devices

We need to understand that the author uses several devices to introduce material in his epistle. In Hebrews 1:4-2:18 the general idea is that Jesus is greater than the angels, but within this general theme he introduces another idea which he will not elaborate upon for another several chapters. He usually does this at the end of the chapter, so be ready for it when we get there: I call it a "hook word" or "billboarding." For example, in chapter 1:14, in talking about angels, the author mentions the idea of angels serving those who are inheriting salvation, this is the "hook" word. In chapter 2 he elaborates not on angels, but he uses the introduction of the word to make a parenthetical statement about salvation.

Salvation: A Warning

> For this reason we must pay much closer attention to what we have heard, so that we do not drift away from it.
> - Hebrews 2:1

We must pay attention to what we have heard and avoid the danger of "drifting away" from it. Like an arrow that slips from the bow or a boat slips past a safe harbor. The idea is of drifting away from truth.

> For if the word spoken through angels proved unalterable, and every transgression and disobedience received a just penalty,
> - Hebrews 2:2

The reason why we must pay closer attention to what was spoken through the angels (spoken by angels to Abraham, spoken to Lot by angels concerning the destruction of Sodom, the Law given to Moses through the angels, Galatians 3:19), was required to be obeyed, and God punished without exception those who disobeyed.

> [3] how will we escape if we neglect so great a salvation? After it was at the first spoken through the Lord, it was confirmed to us by those who heard, [4] God also testifying with them, both by signs and wonders and by various miracles and by gifts of the Holy Spirit according to His own will.
> - Hebrews 2:3-4

How will they escape who neglect the words given by the Son who is higher than angels? Not only spoken by the Son, but preached by the Apostles and confirmed by miracles. If God punished those who disobeyed the word spoken by angels, imagine the result for those who neglect (neglect refers to believers because disbelievers "reject") God's word:

- the word of salvation, forgiveness/eternal life (superior to law)
- spoken by the Son (superior to angels)
- confirmed by Apostles and miracles

The warning is that if even the angels didn't escape punishment, those who neglect the word spoken by Jesus will not escape either. Once the warning is given, the author moves along with his discussion.

Man's Position

He's described Jesus' position above the angels and now will explain why Jesus took, for a while, a position below them - man's position. He does this by first explaining the position that man has according to God.

> For He did not subject to angels the world to come, concerning which we are speaking.
> - Hebrews 2:5

In speaking of man, the author alludes to the fact that in the future man will inherit with Christ a new world order, not the angels! The new heavens and earth where Christ is King and will have His disciples reigning with Him, not the angels.

> [6] But one has testified somewhere, saying,
> "What is man, that You remember him?
> Or the son of man, that You are concerned about him?
> [7] "You have made him for a little while lower than the angels;
> You have crowned him with glory and honor,
> And have appointed him over the works of Your hands;
> [8] You have put all things in subjection under his feet."
> - Hebrews 2:6-8a

The vague introduction here was a common literary device that emphasized divine origin. In modern parlance we would say, "The Bible says..." The Jews were familiar with this psalm (Psalm 8:4-6). The psalm in its original context referred to man and his position in God's creation. Man's original position was at the head of creation, below the angels, with dominion over the earth (Genesis 1:26-30). God isn't putting angels in charge of the world to come, He's putting man - man who was originally in charge of creation.

> For in subjecting all things to him, He left nothing that is not subject to him. But now we do not yet see all things subjected to him.
> - Hebrews 2:8b

This passage summarizes the idea that all things are subject to man. What isn't written but understood is that man fell from this position through sin and his dominion was severely cut back (Genesis 3:16; 17-19). The author says that we don't see man as that ruler now, but he hints at man's return to glory. Also, before describing Jesus' position below the angels for a time, he will first explain man's situation and hope for future return to glory.

Jesus' Position

In the following verses the writer describes Jesus' position and the reasons why He took the low position. In the original context, the psalm in verses 6-8 talked about man, but now the author takes this scripture and shows how Jesus is the ultimate fulfillment of these words. In a historic sense the passage refers to man as a human being, but in a prophetic sense it speaks of Christ. The author now matches the facts of Jesus' life and death to give the passage its prophetic meaning. (Aside from its historic meaning.)

> But we do see Him who was made for a little while lower than the angels, namely, Jesus, because of the suffering of death crowned with glory and honor, so that by the grace of God He might taste death for everyone.
> - Hebrews 2:9

We don't yet see man's glory but we do see Jesus, made for a while like a man (lower than angels). We also see His glory and honor following His death. His death is a "hook word" that will be discussed in a moment. Without mentioning it specifically, the author refers to the resurrection which was the basis of preaching through which his readers originally came to faith. They don't see man's glory, but they see Jesus, like a man, dying and being raised from the dead to a position of glory and honor. The author will show how this will ultimately mean glory and honor for man also, but first he returns to deal with the subject of death that was introduced earlier.

Death for Everyone

The point that the author is making about Jesus' death is that it was an honorable death; one that led to glory. His death was not a deserved death like man's death (men suffer death as a result of their own sin - Romans 6:23). Jesus' death was substitutionary. It was the sin of others that caused his death and so He suffered a personal death for other people's sins. For this reason, He did not suffer a shameful death due to the guilt of personal sin.

This point is important because the death of the Messiah was an obstacle to faith for Jews. The Jewish Messiah was imagined to be a strong leader bringing the nation freedom and prosperity. They stumbled over the fact that Jesus was crucified as a common criminal by a foreign army. This was a very persuasive argument capable of shaking their faith. It is one reason why the author tells them to pay closer attention to the gospel! This is why he mentions that His death was according to the will and purpose of God and was substitutionary in nature.

The author will now explain the relationship between the suffering and death of Jesus and the salvation of man. He does this to make the concept of a "suffering Messiah" acceptable to them. He says three things about the suffering:

1. The suffering was according to God's will

> For it was fitting for Him, for whom are all things, and through whom are all things, in bringing many sons to glory, to perfect the author of their salvation through sufferings.
> - Hebrews 2:10

It was fitting according to God's plan and nature to equip Jesus completely for the task of saving man (bringing sons to glory). In order to save man, death was necessary (he will explain this later). God fully prepared His Son for this suffering by equipping Him with a human body and nature. "Perfect" means to equip completely. The author will go on to say that in His humanity, Jesus was fully human - meaning that He was fully capable of suffering. Jesus is higher and superior to angels, but when He became a man He also fully shared man's inferior position beneath the angels. This was also according to God's will and word.

> For both He who sanctifies and those who are sanctified are all from one Father; for which reason He is not ashamed to call them brethren,
> - Hebrews 2:11

Sanctified means to set aside for a special purpose. God's purpose for us is that we become His children. Because of the sanctification we have obtained through the suffering of Jesus, we have become God's children and, for this reason, Jesus can call us His brethren. He comes down to take on our humanity. In doing so He raises us up to take on His spirituality. In this way we become united having the one Father. He is not ashamed of us. At this point the author will quote several Old Testament passages in order to support the idea that Jesus became fully human:

> saying,
> "I will proclaim Your name to My brethren,
> In the midst of the congregation I will sing Your praise."
> - Hebrews 2:12

This passage comes from Psalm 22:22. It is a prayer asking for deliverance and help, as well as offering praise when the prayer is answered. The author's point being that Jesus also prayed when suffering and now declares salvation among His brethren - like a man.

> And again,
> "I will put My trust in Him."
> And again,
> "Behold, I and the children whom God has given Me."
> - Hebrews 2:13

The Old Testament context comes from Isaiah 8:17-18 where the prophet refers to his two sons. Distressed and rejected by a disobedient people, the prophet expressed these words to affirm his faith in God and looked to his two children as witnesses to the salvation God would bring. The author sees David and Isaiah's words as illustration of higher truths:

- The Messiah's complete trust in God as all men should.

- The Messiah's willingness to associate with God's sons as a human.

The writer puts these words into Jesus' mouth to demonstrate that He responded to God as a human. This is done as a defense against accusations that Jesus was merely a vision or angelic being on earth, and not fully man. He is also echoing John's words in John 1:14, "The Word became flesh and dwelt among us..."

The writer of the Hebrew letter adds several Old Testament passages at this point in order to support the idea that what he is saying was in line with what the prophets said concerning the Messiah, that He would be human and that He would suffer, all according to God's will.

2. The results of suffering

The author has established the idea that the incarnation was according to God's plan and, as man, Jesus was fully human. Now he goes on to explain what Jesus accomplished with His suffering.

> Therefore, since the children share in flesh and blood, He Himself likewise also partook of the same, that through death He might render powerless him who had the power of death, that is, the devil,
> - Hebrews 2:14

He repeats the idea of Jesus' need to become like those He wished to save. He also shows that His death as a human being was necessary in order to destroy Satan's power. Satan has power over death in that he manipulates and seduces man into committing sin, and according to God's Word, sin is punishable by death (Romans 6:23). When it comes to the battle over sin, Satan is more powerful than unregenerated man.

Jesus, on the other hand, was able to resist Satan's attacks and was thus without sin (I Peter 2:22). His death, therefore, was not a punishment for His sins but rather became a payment for the sins of others. We die with a moral debt for sin, and this condition condemns us at judgment. Jesus, on the other hand, dies with no moral debt and so His life offered in death becomes a full payment for the sins of others. Now that there is a payment for sin several things happen:

1. Satan has no power over death because the thing he controls, sin leading to death, now has a neutralizer. Satan continues to lie, seduce and deceive men into sin, but there is now something that removes all sin: the sacrifice of Jesus Christ.

2. Men are free from slavery caused by the fear of death.

> and might free those who through fear of death were subject to slavery all their lives.
> - Hebrews 2:15

Before, there was no solution to sin, and so death was inevitable. Because of Jesus' cross and its payment for sin, men no longer needed to be afraid of the condemnation they faced. There was now a payment for sin. Without condemnation and death as their inevitable end, men were free to be sons of God and take their place with Christ in the heavenly realm.

The third thing the author says regarding Jesus' suffering:

3. The suffering Messiah is the "correct" view of the Jewish Messiah

Remember, the original point in all of this was to show that a suffering Messiah was honorable and legitimate because the idea of Jesus' crucifixion caused much doubt to Jews. In the last verses the author goes on to show that far from being a shameful thing for the Messiah to suffer, it was actually the ultimate fulfillment of every aspect of their Jewish religious system, and a perfect sign that the Messiah could help them now (as they suffered persecution).

> For assuredly He does not give help to angels, but He gives help to the descendant of Abraham.
> - Hebrews 2:16

Jews understood their position below angels, their need for a savior as sinful men and God's promise of salvation. In verse 16 the author establishes that man (Jews in particular) needs salvation and God offered it to them, not angels (final reference to them), and that Jesus' suffering was for them, not angels.

> Therefore, He had to be made like His brethren in all things, so that He might become a merciful and faithful high priest in things pertaining to God, to make propitiation for the sins of the people.
> - Hebrews 2:17

Now he refers to what they knew about how God dealt with sin - by the offering of a sacrifice by a priest (the Jewish sacrificial system). Note that another "hook word" has appeared that he will expand on later: high priest. The priest was a "go-between" or mediator between God and the people. On the one hand, he was human and understood human weakness. On the other, he was set aside for exclusive service by God to offer sacrifices on behalf of the people. The priests served exclusively in the temple. They had no other work nor did they own land or were involved in commerce.

The argument was that Jesus had to become a human and experience suffering and temptation so that, like the priest, He would be able to understand man's weakness and empathize with him. Like the priests, Jesus offered a sacrifice on behalf of the people. Here the author shows how Jesus is similar to the high priest, but later he will demonstrate how Jesus is superior to the high priest. The point in this verse, however, is that according to Jewish religion, a sacrifice for sin was an honorable thing ordained by God in order to deal with sin. The author states that the death of Christ for the sins of men, by comparison, is also an honorable thing totally in line within the Jewish system. Later on he will show how Jesus' sacrifice is superior, but for now he only wants to demonstrate that Jesus' sacrifice is not a shameful thing.

> For since He Himself was tempted in that which He has suffered, He is able to come to the aid of those who are tempted.
> - Hebrews 2:18

At the end of this section there is an exhortation. Since the human Savior suffered (as part of His work to save man from sin) it means that He is able to understand and help with human suffering. He subtly refers to their persecution and reminds them that a suffering savior is well qualified to help them with this burden.

Summary

Within the context of the idea that Jesus is greater than angels, the author introduces the concept that He was also, for a time, lower than angels, and during that time shared not only in human nature but human suffering as well. Without taking his eye off of the ideas that Jesus was the divine son of God and exalted above the angels, the author adds the following things about Jesus when He, for a time, took a position below the angels as a human being:

1. This was according to God's plan. The Messiah had to become human (lower than angels) in order to save man.

2. His suffering produced important and necessary results: A - Destruction of Satan's power over sin and death; B - Freedom for mankind to become children of God.

3. His suffering was in accordance with the basic concepts of the Jewish religion.

We've learned a lot about the theology of Jesus' incarnation and His atonement, and how these were the true fulfillment of Old Testament prophecy as well as the real substance of the Jewish sacrificial system. But we are not Jews, what lessons can we, as modern day Christians draw from all of this?

1. **We must pay attention to what we have heard.** We, today, must also be careful to pay attention to what Jesus teaches lest we drift away from it. They were not paying attention to the Word! They were tempted with arguments that it was shameful for a Messiah to die on the cross. In our age we are tempted to abandon our faith by sophisticated philosophies that repudiate God's Word, cast doubt upon the deity of Christ and the reality of sin, and judgment by scoffers

and mockers. We must pay closer and closer attention to God's Word lest "we" drift away.

2. **We must not be afraid.** God has freed us from sin and death through His elaborate plan in Jesus. We must no longer be afraid of death, sin or failure because we are free from the consequences of these things. We need to learn to live like sons and daughters of God because in Christ we will reach our ultimate potential. Let us not judge ourselves too quickly, let us wait for the end and, if we are faithful, we will wear a crown!

3. **We must put all of our trust in Jesus.** Jesus came to share our human experience so He could effectively help us. How foolish we are when we ignore the Lord who sits above all authority and power in heaven, and rely on other things to rescue us! These Jews were being tempted to return to their temple ritual and law to save themselves from persecution. Little did they know that only a few years after they read this letter, the temple and all that was precious in the Jewish religion was to be utterly destroyed by a Roman army (70 AD).

We need to stop trusting earthly things that will ultimately be destroyed and begin to trust in the only One who can save us from eternal destruction: the glorious Jesus Christ!

CHAPTER 4
JESUS: GREATER THAN MOSES

Hebrews 3:1-4:13

This epistle was written to certain Christian Jews who, because of persecution, were considering a return to their former religion. The author encourages them to be faithful by arguing that Christianity is superior to Judaism and is, in fact, the fulfillment of the Jewish religion. In successive chapters, the author demonstrates how Christ is superior to the Jewish prophets as well as the angels who the Jews held in high esteem as spiritual beings. Once he has done this, the author will go on to compare Jesus to one of the most prestigious Jewish leaders in their history: Moses.

Moses: Background

Moses was born during the Jewish bondage in Egypt in approximately 1500 BC. He was raised by an Egyptian princess who found him hidden in a basket by his mother in an attempt to save his life during a persecution of male children by the Egyptians against the Jewish people. He was educated at the Egyptian court, but at age 40 tried to lead the Jewish people in a revolt, killing an Egyptian in the process. He escaped and lived as a shepherd in the desert for an additional 40 years.

God called him at 80 years of age to return to Egypt and lead the Jewish people out of Egypt to a land originally promised to their ancestor, Abraham. The Lord performed great miracles through Moses and his brother, Aaron, in order to free the people from Egyptian slavery, but their lack of faith and disobedience changed a journey that would have only required several months into a 40 year wandering in the wilderness. During these four decades, however, God through His servant Moses, gave the Jewish people their laws (Ten Commandments), place of worship (Tabernacle), manner of worship (sacrificial system), as well as their religious leaders (priests and Levites) and social customs (food restrictions, festivals, marriage and legal systems). In the desert they became a new and structured society through Moses' leadership. Moses did disobey God, and like the generation that left Egypt with him, did not enter the Promised Land but only saw it from afar before he died. He was, however, considered the greatest of Jewish leaders and a source of authority.

Moses and Christ

In chapter three and part of chapter four, the author compares Christ to Moses. This would be very meaningful to Jewish Christians. The authors of the gospels mention Moses over 80 times, more than any other figure in the Old Testament. Moses was seen as a "type" or "preview" of Christ in the Old Testament, and New Testament writers often pointed this out. For example:

- Moses lifting up the serpent in the desert (Numbers 21:4-9), Jesus being lifted up on the cross (John 3:14)

- Moses giving manna in the desert (Exodus 16), Jesus being the bread of heaven (John 6:3)

- Both threatened to be killed as babies (Exodus 1-2, Matthew 2:16)

- Both deliverers of their people. Both initially rejected (Acts 7:20-44, Romans 9:32)

The author of Hebrews will continue to draw parallels between Jesus and Moses to show Jesus' superiority, and he will draw parallels between their followers as well in order to emphasize the importance of faithfulness.

Outline — 3:1-4:13

The section we are studying has two main parts:

1. A comparison of Moses and Jesus in five areas

    a. Chosen People - Holy Brethren

    b. Promised Land - Celestial Call

    c. Apostle of Liberation - Apostle of Salvation

    d. Related to High Priest - High Priest of Salvation

    e. Servant of House of God - Builder of the House of God

2. A warning to Jesus' followers

Moses' generation did not enter the Promised Land because of disbelief and disobedience. Be careful not to follow their example.

Moses and Jesus: Comparison — 3:1-6a

In the previous chapter the author billboarded the idea that Jesus is like a high priest (faithful and merciful). He'll develop this idea in chapters 4-5, but first he compares Jesus to Moses because Moses appeared historically before the high priest and, as a historical figure, had a greater impact on the Jews than any priest. He also addresses his readers as pilgrims on their way to a heavenly land thus establishing a basis of comparison between themselves, Jesus' followers and Moses' followers who were pilgrims on their way to the Promised Land here on earth.

> [1] Therefore, holy brethren, partakers of a heavenly calling, consider Jesus, the Apostle and High Priest of our confession;

Holy - because they have been sanctified (set apart) by Christ. Brethren - because they have a "brother" in Christ by virtue of His incarnation. Heavenly calling - because they have been called (by the gospel) to come to a "celestial" country - heaven. Our promised land is celestial not geographical. As Christians, we are not nation building or looking for a cultural homeland to call our own here on earth. We are passing through this world on our way to the next world we have been called to by Jesus. Consider Jesus - you who have been called should consider or compare Jesus in light of Moses. See how Jesus compares to him. The author compares three things:

1. The Apostle of our confession. Moses was an apostle (one sent with authority). He gave God's Word to the people and led them to the Promised Land. Jesus is God's messenger who brings freedom from death and eternal salvation. It is Jesus that we confess to be saved, not Moses.

2. The High Priest of our confession. Moses was related
   to the High Priest (he was Aaron's brother) and gave
   him the instructions for the priesthood and the
   sacrificial system. Jesus is the High Priest and by His
   own sacrifice saves us. Jesus is both High Priest and
   sacrifice - an idea that the author is presenting here
   (billboarding), but will explain later on.

3. Faithful – vs. 2-6

> [2] He was faithful to Him who appointed Him, as
> Moses also was in all His house.

Moses was faithful (the author doesn't detract from him). He
was faithful to Israel and to his mission. Jesus was also
faithful, but He had a different role and mission.

> [3] For He has been counted worthy of more glory than
> Moses, by just so much as the builder of the house
> has more honor than the house. [4] For every house is
> built by someone, but the builder of all things is
> God. [5] Now Moses was faithful in all His house as a
> servant, for a testimony of those things which were
> to be spoken later; [6] but Christ was faithful as a Son
> over His house — whose house we are

Moses was faithful as a servant in God's household. He
faithfully delivered the Law without changing it. He was faithful
in his post as leader. He was part of the spiritual temple that
God was building. Jesus, on the other hand, is not a servant
in the house, He is the Son of God over the house. The Law
was His word. He created the people and the nation. He
established the foundation for it with His own blood.

The author says that in His role of Son and builder, Jesus was, like Moses, faithful. However, by virtue of His position in relationship to the house of God, He is greater than Moses ("worthy of more glory" verse 3). We appreciate the house but give the award to the architect. In this sense, as the architect, Jesus is over the household of God, not Moses. The readers of this epistle are tempted to return to Judaism, and Moses was the human embodiment of that religion. The writer demonstrates how Jesus is greater than Moses and now warns them about what a return to Moses would actually mean.

Moses and Jesus: Warning — 3:6b-19

> 6b if we hold fast our confidence and the boast of our hope firm until the end.

The entire warning is summarized here. We are the household, temple and family that God is building and over which He has put Christ.

We continue in this position _if_ (key word) we hold fast (steady, unmoved like a ship in a storm).

Confidence - if we hold fast without fear, panic or complaint, but with confidence.

Boast of our hope - the reason why we hold fast is because we are free from condemnation and the fear of death (Romans 8:1). Biblical hope is confident expectation, not simply "wishing" for something to happen.

Firm until the end - we maintain this firm confidence until death.

The true Christians then and now are those who believe God when He promises eternal life, and they live in such a way that demonstrates belief in that promise until the end. The author moves from this opening comment to give some practical examples of when God's people didn't have this confidence and were unable to maintain their hope, and thus were punished. In this way the author appeals to them through a warning and a promise.

1. A Warning Against Disbelief

The warning is based on Psalm 95:7-11 where the author of the psalm refers to the rebelliousness of the people under Moses:

> [7] Therefore, just as the Holy Spirit says,
> "Today if you hear His voice,
> [8] Do not harden your hearts as when they provoked Me,
> As in the day of trial in the wilderness,
> [9] Where your fathers tried Me by testing Me,
> And saw My works for forty years.

The Hebrew writer compares the Jewish rebellion under Moses to the Jewish Christians contemplating leaving Christ.

> [10] "Therefore I was angry with this generation,
> And said, 'They always go astray in their heart,
> And they did not know My ways';
> [11] As I swore in My wrath,
> 'They shall not enter My rest.'"

God's punishment was to prohibit them from entering the Promised Land (referred to as the "rest").

> [12] Take care, brethren, that there not be in any one of you an evil, unbelieving heart that falls away from the living God.

The warning is to guard against disbelief because it leads to falling away. Here the author equates "falling away" from Christ with falling away from the true and living God.

> [13] But encourage one another day after day, as long as it is still called "Today," so that none of you will be hardened by the deceitfulness of sin.

He says that the root of the problem is sin, and sin leads the way to eventual punishment.

SIN → DISBELIEF → APOSTACY → PUNISHMENT

He exhorts them to encourage each other every day in the battle against sin because then, as now, Christians are tempted every day, and often underestimate the power of sin.

> [14] For we have become partakers of Christ, if we hold fast the beginning of our assurance firm until the end,

He also reminds them that the rewards of hope only go to those who are faithful to the end. We must remain as strong at the end of our lives in Christ as we are at the beginning. In the journey to the heavenly land it is not how fast you travel that is important, it is if you finish the journey faithfully that counts, and daily encouragement is needed to accomplish this. This is why many congregations meet several times per week for worship, fellowship, teaching and encouragement to continue the journey.

[15] while it is said,
"Today if you hear His voice,
Do not harden your hearts, as when they provoked
Me."
[16] For who provoked Him when they had heard?
Indeed, did not all those who came out of Egypt led
by Moses? [17] And with whom was He angry for forty
years? Was it not with those who sinned, whose
bodies fell in the wilderness? [18] And to whom did He
swear that they would not enter His rest, but to those
who were disobedient? [19] So we see that they were
not able to enter because of unbelief.

Here the author gives an instance where the Israelites
perished in the desert as a result of their unfaithfulness. The
point is that their sins didn't disqualify them, it was the
unfaithfulness that their sins caused that led them to failure.
This example is given for his readers who, because of their
disbelief in Christ, are being tempted to abandon the journey
of faith that they are on. He tells them to encourage one
another in this journey so they will finish faithfully. He then
transitions from giving them a warning to describing the
promise that awaits those who are faithful.

2. A Promise of Rest

The promise of heaven was couched in various terms such as
"glory," "eternal life" and "rest." For the Jews of the Old
Testament period, two "types" signified or pointed to a
heavenly reward. One was the Sabbath day, a one day
(Saturday) earthly rest from work in order to concentrate on
one's relationship with God that ultimately pointed to a time in
the future where there would be a never ending time of
unbroken fellowship with Him.

The reason why we, as Christians, do not keep the Sabbath
as the Jewish people did before Christ, is that we have

already begun that unbroken fellowship with God (John 17:21). We do not need to set a 24-hour period aside to symbolize what will eventually arrive with the coming of the Messiah; the Messiah has come (Acts2:1-42)! We are spiritually united to God through Christ, and have knowledge of God through His Word contained in the Bible. We have spiritual regeneration through the Holy Spirit (Romans 8:11-12). Faithful Jews before Christ, the Jewish Christians that the author was addressing as well as ourselves today, are enjoying the everlasting Sabbath rest and will do so if we are faithful to the end.

Another type for the heavenly reward was the Promised Land, which was to be the homeland for God's people, but also pointed to the establishment of the kingdom of God on earth. That kingdom was not meant to be political or geographical, but spiritual. Christ established it with His death and resurrection, and all who believe and obey the gospel enter into it (John 3:5). In this passage, therefore, the author mixes these images saying that the "rest" was to be had in the "promised land." The Jews looked forward to a rest/renewal when they reached the promised land (Canaan), but most did not make it because of disbelief and died in the desert as a result. The writer uses the spiritual meaning of these words to tell his readers that they will not reach their reward of heaven either, and for the same reason.

> [1] Therefore, let us fear if, while a promise remains of entering His rest, any one of you may seem to have come short of it.

The promise is still before them, but they should be frightened if they're falling back from it through disbelief.

> [2] For indeed we have had good news preached to us, just as they also; but the word they heard did not

profit them, because it was not united by faith in
those who heard.

He suggests that the problem in the desert was the people's
doubt that God could actually bring them to the promised
land; that such a place even existed. Christians, like the
Israelites, had received a "promise of rest" contained in the
gospel. However, they should take care not to act like the
Israelites who didn't enter because they heard but didn't
continue believing and thus did not complete the journey.

[3] For we who have believed enter that rest, just as
He has said,
"As I swore in My wrath,
They shall not enter My rest,"
although His works were finished from the foundation
of the world. [4] For He has said somewhere
concerning the seventh day: "And God rested on the
seventh day from all His works"; [5] and again in this
passage, "They shall not enter My rest." [6] Therefore,
since it remains for some to enter it, and those who
formerly had good news preached to them failed to
enter because of disobedience, [7] He again fixes a
certain day, "Today," saying through David after so
long a time just as has been said before,
"Today if you hear His voice,
Do not harden your hearts."
[8] For if Joshua had given them rest, He would not
have spoken of another day after that.

Those who believe need to understand that the "rest" is still
available to those who persevere. It has not been withdrawn
despite the failure of some to enter in because of disbelief. In
other words, the Promised Land is still there spiritually. He
quotes a passage from the Psalms written long after events in

the desert took place showing that the "rest" God offered the Jews was still present in David's day, 500 years after Moses.

The idea was that the "rest" was not only for Moses' generation, but for every generation who would believe. So long as it is today, the "rest" is there. He then quotes Joshua and says that if Joshua's conquest of the land would have fulfilled the promise of "rest," then David would not be talking about it as a possibility centuries later. The promise remained alive. Unlike the Jews who thought that in entering and possessing the land of Canaan, they had received everything; the author is saying that the best is yet to come!

> [9] So there remains a Sabbath rest for the people of God. [10] For the one who has entered His rest has himself also rested from his works, as God did from His.

He confirms that the promise of rest remains. He explains that the promise is not something you own, it is something you enter into. What you enter into is not described, only that it will be different than here. So, to Christian Jews who are discouraged doubting that the suffering is not worth the goal or that the goal is even out there, the writer assures them that as God rested from His work, so will His people.

Warning Summarized — 4:11-13

> [11] Therefore let us be diligent to enter that rest, so that no one will fall, through following the same example of disobedience.

'Please don't repeat the mistake of the Israelites,' he says. You Christians are in the process of entering into the rest, don't fall back because of disobedience which will lead to disbelief, apostasy and failure. Be diligent (zealous) to enter into that rest. It is interesting to note that later on he will warn that falling away from church attendance is the first sign of eventually falling away from Christ.

> [12] For the word of God is living and active and sharper than any two-edged sword, and piercing as far as the division of soul and spirit, of both joints and marrow, and able to judge the thoughts and intentions of the heart. [13] And there is no creature hidden from His sight, but all things are open and laid bare to the eyes of Him with whom we have to do.

Listen to the warning because it comes from God's word, which is power and not to be ignored. He makes several comparisons to show that the Word has power. He describes it as being living, active or like a sharp sword.

For example, he couples words together like soul and spirit, joint and marrow, thoughts and intentions. Only something very sharp could divide these things or lay the heart bare, since nothing can be hidden from God's word. Although the chapter doesn't end here, the thought ends here. The example, warnings and punishments concerning disobedience and disbelief should be heeded because His promises and punishments are absolutely sure and as real for us today as it was for them.

Summary

The author begins by comparing Moses and Jesus along different lines to demonstrate that Moses, even as a faithful servant and leader of the Jews, is not comparable to Jesus who saves souls and actually builds the household of God which Moses only served. He goes on to warn them that they will fail to reach their goal (heaven) for the same reasons that Moses and the Israelites failed to reach their goal (land of Canaan): disobedience and disbelief, so be careful. He reassures them that the "rest" or "promise" is still before them and worthy of the sacrifice and perseverance in every generation. Jesus never said it would be easy to continue believing until the end. He promised, however, that it would be worth the effort.

CHAPTER 5
JESUS: GREATER THAN AARON
PART 1

Hebrews 4:14-5:10

In his argument encouraging Jewish Christians to remain faithful to Christ, the author of the book of Hebrews divides his letter into two sections:

1. He shows that the glory of Christ is greater than the glory of the Jewish religion and all of its parts. In the last several chapters we have covered three of these parts: the Jewish prophets, the Jewish concept of angels, and one of the great Jewish leaders, Moses.

2. In the second section the author will talk about the glory of the church (Jesus' body) and what keeps it glorious.

In this chapter we will examine what he says about the fourth part of the Jewish religion: the priesthood and, especially, the High Priest. This is a long passage where the writer will touch on three specific topics:

1. Jesus as High Priest, greater than Aaron, the first High Priest appointed by God through Moses.

2. The writer again rebukes and warns his readers concerning unfaithfulness. He admonishes them not to abandon the superior High Priest who is Jesus. There is none greater than Him.

3. Jesus is a different kind of high priest (not like Aaron, but rather like Melchizedek).

Jesus is a High Priest — Hebrews 4:14-5:10

In the previous section the author was reminding his readers not to ignore the warning contained in God's Word concerning disobedience and disbelief. He told them that because of this, Moses' followers had not entered their "rest" in the promised land. The suggestion was that they were in danger of the same fate if they disbelieved and disobeyed their leader, Jesus, and would not enter the true promised land and true rest which was heaven.

Bridge

In verses 14-16 he changes gears and encourages them to renew their efforts to go forward towards this rest/promise because they have a helper who is already there awaiting them and helping them to enter in. This is the key idea in this section. It is with this device that the author introduces the idea that Jesus is also a high priest. He boldly makes his summary idea in one concise statement.

> [14] Therefore, since we have a great high priest who has passed through the heavens, Jesus the Son of God, let us hold fast our confession.

1. Christians have a great high priest. No Jewish high priest is referred to as great. The unspoken suggestion was that the Jewish religion was superior because it had a priestly system. Priests who could go before God on behalf of the people to thank, make requests and atone for sin. The author states that Christians also have a high priest.

2. The Christian's high priest is in heaven. While Jewish priests served here on earth, the Christian's representative is in heaven appealing to God on his behalf.

3. Jesus is that high priest. He is the Son of God and serves as high priest for His people.

4. The people should be encouraged. If their high priest is already in heaven, they need to maintain their faith.

> [15] For we do not have a high priest who cannot sympathize with our weaknesses, but One who has been tempted in all things as we are, yet without sin.

Even though Jesus, as Son of God and high priest, is in heaven with God, this does not mean He cannot relate to the problems of human suffering and failure. He, as a man, was tested by Satan and by the limits of humanity and did not sin. The suggestion is that in Him we have the perfect mediator. One who can understand and sympathize with our weaknesses but, at the same time, can stand boldly before God on man's behalf because He Himself has no guilt or condemnation due to sin.

> [16] Therefore let us draw near with confidence to the throne of grace, so that we may receive mercy and find grace to help in time of need.

Since Jesus knows the power of sin (He was tested), the weakness of men (He was fully human) and the mercy of God (He had a divine nature), His followers can approach God with confidence. He has gone before them and prepared the way and now tells them that if they come in His name, they will find mercy and God's help when they need it.

Introduction to Aaron — Hebrews 5:1-4

In chapter five the author introduces Aaron, Moses' brother, who was the first high priest. If he is to make a comparison to Jesus, he needs to describe who Aaron was and what he did. Originally, the ones who offered sacrifices to God as a form of worship were the heads of families. We often read about instances where Abraham, Isaac, Jacob and their sons offered animal sacrifices to thank or make pledges to God (Genesis 12:7-8; Genesis 35:7). The basic idea behind a sacrifice of any kind was that something was transferred from the physical realm to the spiritual realm through death or destruction. Death or destruction was the passageway from this dimension to the spiritual or unseen dimension. For example:

- Adam and Eve - Atonement for sin transferred from them to God through death of an animal (Genesis 3:21).

- Noah - Thanksgiving for safety through flood transferred from earth to heaven by animal sacrifice (Genesis 8:20).

- Jacob - Vow to have only God as his God transferred to spiritual realm by pouring out (destroying) oil on a pillar (Genesis 28:18).

When God gave the Law to Moses, He also included a more formalized system of sacrifices that contained specific instructions concerning the reasons, times, manners and materials to be used in the practice of sacrifice. Much of this information is contained in the book of Leviticus. The Jewish religious system of worship was built around the activity of sacrificing to God a variety of animals and produce in order to express (transfer from physical to spiritual) different things. Sacrifices that expressed thanksgiving, purification, atonement, blessing, etc. In Leviticus 1:6 we read the instructions for the preparation of sacrifices such as burnt offerings, peace offerings, sin offerings and guilt offerings, to name a few.

God provided the details concerning the killing and preparation of the animal, how to actually offer the sacrifice, the order in which it was to be presented, and what other items were to accompany the sacrifice. It was complex, demanding, expensive and time consuming. Some sacrifices had to be done every day, others on special occasions. In addition to these, the priests had to offer the sacrifices that the people brought to them as well.

God also appointed a specific person and family to carry out these tasks, as well as a specific place where things were to be done (tabernacle/temple). Aaron, Moses' brother from the tribe of Levi, along with his sons were the first ones appointed by God to this role. Sacrificing would no longer be done by the heads of each family, but by a high priest on behalf of all the families. The important point to remember here is that this task/ministry was only given to Aaron and his sons and their descendants. According to God's Law, only the descendants of Aaron could serve as priests. This is why they called it the Aaronic priesthood. The high priest also had an elaborate rite of purification and dress that we read about in Leviticus 8:6-9,

^{6} Then Moses had Aaron and his sons come near and washed them with water. ^{7} He put the tunic on him and girded him with the sash, and clothed him with the robe and put the ephod on him; and he girded him with the artistic band of the ephod, with which he tied it to him. ^{8} He then placed the breastpiece on him, and in the breastpiece he put the Urim and the Thummim. ^{9} He also placed the turban on his head, and on the turban, at its front, he placed the golden plate, the holy crown, just as the Lord had commanded Moses.

- **Turban/crown** — He wore a turban made of linen with a blue laced ribbon which held a golden plate which had the words, "HOLINESS TO THE LORD." This was a constant reminder of his separation and calling to serve God and the people (Exodus 28:36-38).

- **Onyx stones** — One stone on each shoulder secured by a strap that served to hold the front and back of the checkered and embroidered ephod. The names of six tribes of Israel were engraved on each stone. Names placed in order of birth (six oldest on the right and six youngest on the left - Josephus). This meant that the high priest carried the names of the tribes before the Lord when ministering in their name (Exodus 26:6-14).

- **Braided chains** — These were made of gold and, along with the ribbons, were used to hold the breastplate in place. The breastplate had rings in each corner and the chains were attached from these to the shoulder plates that held the onyx stones (Exodus 28:14).

- **Breastplate** — This was a piece of elaborately finished cloth of the same material as the ephod. It was twice as long as it was wide but folded over to form a square (about 9"X9") and provide an inner pocket or pouch. As I said, it had rings in each corner from which chains and ribbons were attached to secure it into place. On the breastplate were fastened 12 precious stones (sardius, topaz, emerald, turquoise, sapphire, diamond, jacinth, agate, amethyst, beryl, onyx and jasper) all set in gold. On each stone was engraved the name of one of the tribes of Israel. The idea was that the people and their needs were always close to the high priest's heart and before the Lord constantly (Exodus 28:15-29).

- **Urim/thummin** — Urim = lights / thummin = perfection. It is thought that there were precious gems placed inside the pocket of the breastplate. Not much is known about these, but since this was before the time of prophets, it may be that the priest used these in some way to discern a "yes" or "no" answer from the Lord (Exodus 28:30; Numbers 27:31).

- **Ephod** — An over-garment made of linen with gold, blue, purple and scarlet threading. It was woven together and worn as a tunic. It had a front and back panel and held together by the gold clasps on the shoulders that had the onyx stones (Exodus 28:6-14).

- **Sash/girdle** — The sash/girdle held the ephod in place securely tied. When the high priest was "girded" or "sashed" it meant he was fully clothed in all of his high priestly attire. It was made of golden threads as well as blue, purple, and scarlet linen (Exodus 28:6-14).

- **Robe** — Was worn under the ephod. It was a plain blue sleeveless garment, reinforced at the neck. It extended below the ephod (Exodus 28:31-35).

- **Bells** — Bells of gold were sewn on the hem and could be heard as the priest moved about. The people could know that the high priest had not been struck dead while in the service of the Lord and their offering was acceptable (Exodus 28:35).

- **Pomegranates** — A row of pomegranates were embroidered on the hem of the robe in between the bells. They symbolized fruitfulness (abundant seeds) and God's word as sweet and pleasant food (Exodus 39:24).

- **Tunic** — Basic linen tunic as undergarment. (Leviticus 8:6-9)

- **Barefoot** — The high priest wore no shoes when entering the holy place because this was considered holy ground.

And so, when the author speaks of the high priest, this is the grand image that his readers have of this person, his exalted position and his ministry.

[1] For every high priest taken from among men is appointed on behalf of men in things pertaining to God, in order to offer both gifts and sacrifices for sins; [2] he can deal gently with the ignorant and misguided, since he himself also is beset with weakness; [3] and because of it he is obligated to offer sacrifices for sins, as for the people, so also for himself. [4] And no one takes the honor to himself, but receives it when he is called by God, even as Aaron was.

After reviewing the history and work of the Aaronic priesthood, he notes that they were not all selected on the basis of merit, but rather by the will of God. The author also reminds them that even the priests had to, in the course of their temple service, offer sacrifice for themselves because they also were weak and sinful people, just like the people they represented before God. The idea was that in this way they could understand and sympathize with the people they served. Even Aaron, the first high priest appointed by God, was a weak and sinful man.

Jesus is also a High Priest

The author has already stated this, but in these verses he shows that Jesus has better qualifications to be a high priest than Aaron and his descendants. He mentions two things:

1. Jesus was appointed High Priest

> ⁵ So also Christ did not glorify Himself so as to become a high priest, but He who said to Him,
> "You are My Son,
> Today I have begotten You";
> ⁶ just as He says also in another passage,
> "You are a priest forever
> According to the order of Melchizedek."

Just as Aaron was appointed by God, so was Jesus. He proves his point by quoting two Old Testament scriptures that speak of the Messiah/Son of God and His position (Psalm 2:17; 110:4). The idea is that the Messiah was to be a priest forever, appointed by God along the lines of an Old Testament priest called Melchizedek, not Aaron. In other words, Jesus traces His priestly lineage back to Melchizedek (a person who existed before Aaron), not Aaron. The writer does not explain who this Melchizedek is right away, he merely establishes Christ's appointment as high priest and His lineage. The author knew that for Jews, another stumbling block to accepting Jesus as a high priestly mediator was that He was descended through His earthly father, Joseph, through the line of Judah, not Levi, where the Aaronic priests came from. He will explain the significance of this lineage later.

2. He was Qualified

> [7] In the days of His flesh, He offered up both prayers and supplications with loud crying and tears to the One able to save Him from death, and He was heard because of His piety. [8] Although He was a Son, He learned obedience from the things which He suffered. [9] And having been made perfect, He became to all those who obey Him the source of eternal salvation, [10] being designated by God as a high priest according to the order of Melchizedek.

In order to qualify as a priest you needed to be appointed by God so as to have a right to stand before Him, and you needed to be able to relate to those whom you represented. Aaron qualified in both respects because he was appointed through Moses, and he was human.

In this section the author shows that in addition to His divine appointment, Jesus qualified as one who knew the sufferings of men because He also suffered greatly. He suffered anguish in the garden before His death and, like all men, prayed to God with tears to help Him in His hour of trial. He suffered the restrictions of a human nature and did only what the Father instructed, thus demonstrating that He knew how to obey. He was never morally imperfect, but His human nature was brought totally into submission to God's will, even to the point of death. This is the kind of perfection/maturity revealed here.

Jesus qualified as a priest because He was appointed by God to serve in this way, and He, like Aaron, knew well the sufferings and limitations of the human nature (unlike Aaron however, He was perfect - no sin). The author makes his point in verses 9b-10. Because Jesus is qualified in this way, He is able to perform the priestly duties which will result not only in the temporary helping of His people (which is what happened with Aaron and his descendants, and which he will explain at length later), but Jesus is able to give them an eternal, complete salvation. He reiterates the idea of Melchizedek here as a kind of a "book-end" device to round out his opening remarks that revolved around this mysterious character: Melchizedek.

Summary

1. The author encourages his readers to strive for their hope of rest in heaven assured by the fact that their Lord, Jesus, is already there appealing to God on their behalf as High Priest.

2. He reviews the original qualifications for the high priesthood as regards Aaron, the original high priest of Israel. He had to be appointed by God and sympathetic to the people.

3. He shows them that Jesus is qualified to be high priest because, as Messiah, He was appointed by God to this office. His priesthood, however, was to be eternal in nature (lineage of Melchizedek), not the temporary lineage of Aaron. Also, as one who took on a human nature, Jesus was able to relate to the sufferings of the people He ministered to. The author's conclusion is that because of His qualifications, Christians can have confidence in Jesus as their high priest who ministers in heaven on their behalf. By implication the author is saying that the priesthood of Aaron has been replaced by a greater and the more effective one of Jesus. He will explain how and why later.

Although not fully explained yet, the author reassures all Christians in every era that they have someone already in heaven who is pleading their case at the throne of God. What does this spiritual reality mean for us? It means that we need to pray with this idea in mind and not put off dealing with sin because our high priest is in heaven pleading on our behalf. We can be sure that our sins will be dealt with effectively. Finally, we should always approach God with confidence in all matters because we have been assured that we will find grace and mercy there, not condemnation.

CHAPTER 6
JESUS: GREATER THAN AARON
PART 2

Hebrews 5:11-6:20

The author of the book of Hebrews is comparing Jesus to various aspects of the Jewish religion in order to encourage his readers not to abandon their new faith in Christ for their old faith of Judaism. The notion that the Jewish religion is superior because it boasts of the ancient priesthood of Aaron is dealt with by showing that, in Christ, his readers also have a high priest.

1. He is a legitimate high priest and qualified to be so because like all high priests He has been appointed by God and He can relate to human weakness.

2. He is superior to Aaron because He is already in heaven (by virtue of His resurrection and ascension)

and He comes from the eternal order of Melchizedek, not the temporal order of Aaron.

3. This should give all believers confidence to come to God without fear because their high priest is already in heaven on their behalf and He understands perfectly their weaknesses.

He begins and finishes the passage with a reference to Melchizedek, a mysterious figure who appears only once in the Old Testament, and uses this as a launching pad to rebuke them concerning their immaturity.

Rebuke — Hebrews 5:11-6:20

Admonishment Concerning Their Immaturity

The author rebukes his readers for failing in two areas: the inability to discern truth from error and the failure to have matured into teachers. The reason for this is immaturity caused by a loss of the desire to "hear" the Word (listen with the intent of obeying with all of one's heart).

> [11] Concerning him we have much to say, and it is hard to explain, since you have become dull of hearing.

He picks up on the theme of Melchizedek from the last section and comments that this concept of Jesus' priesthood based on the type of Melchizedek is an important subject with many implications, but they seem unable to grasp it because they are not "hearing" like they used to. Here, he states the case and the reason; in the next three verses he gives the details of their failure.

[12] For though by this time you ought to be teachers, you have need again for someone to teach you the elementary principles of the oracles of God, and you have come to need milk and not solid food.

They have received much teaching and should by this time be able to teach others. Instead, they need again to be taught the ABC's (elementary principles) of the faith (oracles of God). Milk and solid food is a contrast used to refer to mature teachings and basic teachings in the Christian faith.

[13] For everyone who partakes only of milk is not accustomed to the word of righteousness, for he is an infant. [14] But solid food is for the mature, who because of practice have their senses trained to discern good and evil.

One grows in his ability to grasp the more mature matters of the faith by training himself to choose the right way to act and choose this consistently. This learning process begins with the proper response to the ABC's of the faith with movement towards maturity. The author is telling them that because they are still practicing the ABC's of faith (not discerning well and choosing consistently right over wrong, truth from error) they are immature, and he has trouble communicating with them about more mature matters, like the teaching on the person and purpose of Melchizedek.

[1] Therefore leaving the elementary teaching about the Christ, let us press on to maturity, not laying again a foundation of repentance from dead works and of faith toward God, [2] of instruction about washings and laying on of hands, and the resurrection of the dead and eternal judgment. [3] And this we will do, if God permits.

He encourages them to settle, once for all, the elementary teachings and their response to these, and go on to more mature teachings. The teaching about Christ encompasses all of these other teachings. These include what they were taught concerning the person of Christ; repentance and one's attitude towards sin; the working, meaning and necessity of faith; "washings" refer to the various water rituals; the purpose and meaning of the "laying on of hands"; the difference between John and Jesus' baptisms; the resurrection, judgment and matters concerning the end times. These constitute basic Christian teachings, and until a Christian understands, accepts and responds to them in a consistently appropriate way, there can be no growth or teaching of more mature matters.

These Christians were inconsistent. They still were not sure of the deity of Christ. They were being careless with sin and had a worldly attitude. They wanted to go back to their old faith, not yet sure that Christ's baptism washed away all sin so that there was no further need for sacrifice. They were not convinced that at the end Christ would return and judge all men. For these reasons the author calls upon them to make up their minds about these things once and for all so they can go on to other matters. His rebuke is that because they are not settled on these basic teachings, they themselves are not teaching others but need to be taught again, and he will do it if God allows (the opportunity and time). What are the more mature matters? Using the Word to build one another up in Christ, and winning others for Christ.

Warning Against Falling Away

The author makes clear the reason why they must press ahead to maturity. Not to go forward means that they are falling back, and to do so is fatal. The next four verses contain one of the most severe warnings to Christians contained in the New Testament. It is evident that he is talking to Christians because of the way he refers to them. He says that it is possible to fall to such an extent that it becomes impossible to repent.

> [4] For in the case of those who have once been enlightened and have tasted of the heavenly gift and have been made partakers of the Holy Spirit, [5] and have tasted the good word of God and the powers of the age to come,

He says four things that demonstrate that he is talking to Christians:

1. "once been enlightened" - Coming to Christ, knowing the gospel, responding to it is the very essence of enlightenment (John 3:19-22). Only Christians have this kind of enlightenment.

2. "tasted of the heavenly gift" - He is describing the relief, joy and assurance of salvation. Our experience of salvation causes joy (Acts 8:38-39). This is uniquely a Christian's experience.

3. "partakers of the Holy Spirit" - At baptism we receive the gift of the Holy Spirit (Acts 2:38). As Christians we experience His comfort in our lives in a variety of ways: through prayer (Romans 8:26), the struggle/victory over sin (Romans 8:13).

4. "tasted the good word...powers of the age to come" - The author refers to the experience a Christian has in hearing and responding to God's word. Seeing the power it has to transform him into a mature spiritual being. In addition to this, in the first century many Christians exercised miraculous powers - powers that belonged to the Christian age (age to come) which would ultimately be consummated by Christ's return.

> [6a] and then have fallen away, it is impossible to renew them again to repentance,

The experiences that he is referring to can only be had by Christians. He says that Christians who experience these things and then fall back are in great danger of never being renewed again. He says that it becomes impossible for them to repent. It is important to note that the author is referring to the sin of apostasy (abandoning the faith) not morality.

> *"It is one thing to yield to sin contrary to the teachings of our new life in Christ, it is quite another to abandon that new life altogether"*
> *(N. Lightfoot - Commentary on Hebrews pp.126).*

The idea is that a person who practices his faith and repeatedly abandons it and then takes it up again only to reject it once more eventually becomes so hard hearted that he is beyond having any more convictions concerning spiritual life, and thus beyond repentance. He gets to a point where he cannot repent even if he wanted to.

> [6b] since they again crucify to themselves the Son of God, and put Him to open shame.

Their crime is enormous. He visualizes their sin by saying that they take Christ into their hearts at conversion, taste the joy of salvation bought with His blood, share the Spirit, see the change and then tear Him out of their hearts to put Him back on the cross to open shame. The idea of "crucifying to themselves" suggests that they do this to their own harm, not to Jesus'. This type of repeated sin hardens the heart to a point where it can no longer respond to the Word in order to repent.

> [7] For ground that drinks the rain which often falls upon it and brings forth vegetation useful to those for whose sake it is also tilled, receives a blessing from God; [8]but if it yields thorns and thistles, it is worthless and close to being cursed, and it ends up being burned.

At this point the author uses familiar imagery to describe the fate of these: ground that is prepared, receives rain and brings forth produce is blessed by God (it continues to be farmed). That same ground, however, receiving the same care, should it bring up useless thorns and thistles ends up being burned and receives a curse (it is abandoned).

Christians who grow in wisdom, knowledge and maturity will be blessed by God. If they continually rebel, fall back and refuse to produce good spiritual fruit they will be punished and abandoned.

Encouragement

After warning them against falling away, he comforts and encourages them to "hang on to hope." This is the "hook" word that brings us to the next section.

1. Be Faithful

> [9] But, beloved, we are convinced of better things concerning you, and things that accompany salvation, though we are speaking in this way.

Even though he is speaking harshly, he is convinced that they are not yet apostate, but in danger of it. He believes that they are producing the fruit of salvation.

¹⁰ For God is not unjust so as to forget your work and the love which you have shown toward His name, in having ministered and in still ministering to the saints.

These Jewish Christians had helped Gentile believers who were persecuted, and the writer comments that God also sees this and will remember it. There will be more details given about this in chapter 10:32-34.

¹¹ And we desire that each one of you show the same diligence so as to realize the full assurance of hope until the end.

They had been delinquent in good works and love. He encourages them to exercise the same diligence in their faith towards Christ so that their "hope" (eternal glory), which is based on Him, will be fully realized. And this diligence is to be displayed until the end. Their hope for salvation was directly linked to their faith in Christ. As their faith in Him dimmed, so did their hope of salvation. They needed to keep one strong in order to maintain the other.

¹² that you may not be sluggish, but imitators of those who through faith and patience inherit the promises.

They needed to do this in order to inherit the promises, just like those who came before them required perseverance and faithfulness to receive their promises. The point he makes is that they should imitate those people in the past who were not sluggish or lazy. In this section he comforts them by commending the good they have done and encourages them to exercise the same kind of perseverance and faithfulness to Christ if they want to inherit the promises like the heroes of old (a billboard word bridging to chapter 11). For the moment, he mentions one of these heroes of faith: Abraham.

2. God's Oath to Abraham

> [13] For when God made the promise to Abraham, since He could swear by no one greater, He swore by Himself, [14]saying, 'I WILL SURELY BELSS YOU, AND I WILL SURELY MULTIPLY YOU." [15]And thus, having patiently waited, he obtained the promise.

God promised that He would bless Abraham, that through his descendants (and he would have many) all nations would be blessed (Genesis 12:4). It took a long time for this promise to even begin to materialize. Abraham wandered; waited a lifetime before Isaac was born; even had to agree to sacrifice him (the quote here taken from this time).

Divine beings don't need to make oaths, but to reassure men who do, God swore by Himself as His own witness (no one greater) in order to guarantee this promise to Abraham. The promise to Abraham was only fulfilled with the coming of Christ, thousands of years later (Galatians 3:14, 16, 29), but Abraham received a glimpse of the development of the promise as Isaac was born, was rescued from certain death and then was married. Abraham saw this fulfillment in the same way one could see, in the early sprouting of a young tree, its future maturity and glory. Through faith and perseverance, he saw the initial fulfillment of his hope and was overjoyed (John 8:56; Romans 4:20-21).

3. Oaths in General

The author talks about oaths in general and the specific oath that guarantees their salvation.

> [16] for men swear by one greater than themselves, and with them an oath given as confirmation is an end of every dispute.

In general, an oath is taken by calling on a witness greater than self: parents, state or Deity in order to verify the truth or legality of a matter. When there is a dispute or bargaining, once the oath is taken, it is a confirmation that the matter is settled.

> [17] In the same way God, desiring even more to show to the heirs of the promise the unchangeableness of His purpose, interposed with an oath

In this case, the promise made to Abraham by God reaching down to all of his descendants is secure (Christians are spiritual descendants of Abraham - Galatians 3:7), and to reassure them, God used the human device of making an oath as a guarantee that the matter was closed and the promise was absolutely sure. The descendants of Abraham will be blessed because God promised and then vowed to keep His promise.

> [18] in order that by two unchangeable things, in which it is impossible for God to lie, we may have strong encouragement, we who have fled for refuge in laying hold of the hope set before us.

Their vision of salvation was growing dim, and like sailors trying to reach a safe harbor in the storm, they were becoming discouraged of even making it. The author closes this section by saying that salvation (their hope/harbor) is sure because of two things:

1. God is the one who promised it and He never breaks His promises.

2. God has made an oath on the matter and it is impossible for God to lie.

Therefore, he encourages them to be faithful and thus keep their hope in full view because that hope has been promised and guaranteed by God Himself.

4. Relationship Between Hope / Faith / Christ

> [19] This hope we have as an anchor of the soul, a hope both sure and steadfast and one which enters within the veil

Our "hope" is that we will be with God. It is this hope that steadies our souls during times of crisis (anchors steady ships and prevents them from drifting). This hope that Christians have is not wishful thinking. It is sure because it has been promised and guaranteed by God Himself. Even in sickness or pain when we cannot think, pray or even confess our faith, the hope is still sure. It is a hope which expects the greatest of treasures: to be with God, to live forever and to have eternal joy.

"Enters within the veil" - This was a reference to the temple in Jerusalem where the Jews worshipped. It was divided into two main compartments; one part was called the "Holy Place" and was accessible to any qualified priest at any time, the other part, the "Holy of Holies," was separated by a veil and could only be entered once per year by the High Priest on the sacred Day of Atonement when he would offer sacrifice for the sins of the people.

The temple, and more specifically, the Holy of Holies, was the place where God dwelt and all the symbolism of the architecture reinforced the concept that men could not enter and be with God. There was limited access and only by a chosen and highly qualified few (Numbers 6:13). The Levites, who carried the articles of the tabernacle in the desert, were not even allowed to look at the utensils, candlesticks and other items in the Holy of Holies. This under pain of death!

The substance of the hope that the author spoke of was that all men could have free access to God at any time. This is expressed with the image of ordinary people freely entering beyond the veil, into the Holy of Holies. Hope has been personified in Christ as entering the inner sanctuary and bringing His followers with Him to be with God. This is the hope of the Christian, explained to a Jewish mind using Jewish religious ideas.

> [20] where Jesus has entered as a forerunner for us, having become a high priest forever according to the order of Melchizedek.

With this verse the author answers an important question: Why should they have hope? It is the conclusion of this section and the bridge or hook to the next. The reason hope is possible is that Jesus, the High Priest like Melchizedek, has entered the Holy of Holies as a forerunner. This answers the question, "Why do we have hope to enter into the presence of God?"

The Jewish High Priest was a representative of the people and entered the Holy of Holies once per year because the people themselves could not enter in (they were unclean sinners). Jesus, however, is a forerunner. He goes not only to represent but also to prepare the way so that all of His followers can go into the presence of God (a function that the human high priest did not and could not have). Christians have hope (confident expectation) because God has promised to bless them, confirmed this promise with an oath and sent Jesus as a forerunner to guarantee their place with Him in heaven. This hope is always in view (giving joy and peace to the soul) so long as faith remains in Christ, but it fades as faith fades.

Summary

The author encourages these Jewish Christians by confirming that they are not apostate and have been faithful in the past. He reminds them to imitate the lives of the faithful in the past as they remain true to Christ. He uses Abraham as an example of faithfulness and reviews with them the idea of oaths and how God has confirmed His promise with an oath to ultimately save them (there is nothing as sure as a promise from God). Finally, he assures them that their faith in Christ will ultimately result in their hope of salvation being realized, and explains why this is so (their high priest is already in heaven as a forerunner preparing a place for them).

These people were losing hope, enthusiasm and a vision of heaven which was their source of joy and motivation. This was happening, not because of trials or lack of intelligence, but because their faith in Christ was weakening. Faith and hope are linked. Without hope we have no joy, no desire to grow, no enthusiasm for service, no peace, no satisfaction and no salvation. This is because without faith in Jesus, we lose hope which in turn leads to the loss of these other things. His readers were losing hope because their faith was growing weak. The reason for their loss of faith was that they were becoming dull of hearing the words or teachings of Christ (Romans 10:17).

The lesson for us today is that if we don't hear the words of Christ often, we cannot build our faith. If our faith is weak, our hope is dim. If our hope is dim, we cannot experience the joy, peace and anticipation of the heavenly reward that God has promised and guaranteed to us with an oath. This explains why the church is, at times, immature and weak - we lose sight of our hope because our faith is not strong.

Based on this passage let us remember two important things:

1. Every time you wonder if you should come to church service and hear God's Word or not, ask yourself the following questions, "Do I want to build my faith or diminish it? Do I want my hope to increase or decrease?"

2. Remember that the promise of heaven is sure and guaranteed by God's Word and oath. Christ has gone ahead to prepare a place for us (not just any room or the outside courtyard of the Temple where ordinary Jews were restricted because they were not worthy to come any closer to God) inside the Holy of Holies where God dwells. That will be the place for those who maintain a strong faith and do not lose their hope of heaven.

CHAPTER 7
JESUS: GREATER THAN AARON
PART 3

Hebrews 7

In the last three chapters of the book of Hebrews the author has demonstrated how Jesus, as High Priest, was superior to the Aaronic line of high priests in Judaism. The idea was that formerly, under the Mosaic system, the hope of the Jewish people was based on the fact that their priests could go before God and intervene on their behalf (give thanks, appeal for forgiveness, offer praise, etc.).

The author makes the argument that Christians have a better hope because they have a better "type" of high priest in Jesus. He explains that Jesus is in the mold and character of a different kind of high priest; not like Aaron who died and needed a continued lineage to carry on his work; but like Melchizedek who was an "eternal" type and figure in the Old Testament. In this chapter, therefore, the author will elaborate on the person of Melchizedek and Jesus' relationship to him. Keep in mind that the author has explained to his readers that these ideas and teachings were the "meat" of the word, not "milk," meaning that these ideas were part of the more mature teachings about Christianity and not for the immature.

Background of Melchizedek — Hebrews 7:1-28

Before we look at Jesus' relationship to Melchizedek we need to review the passage that refers to this person.

> [11]Then they took all the goods of Sodom and Gomorrah and all their food supply, and departed. [12]And they also took Lot, Abram's nephew, and his possessions and departed, for he was living in Sodom.
> - Genesis 14:11-12

There was a local war between rival kings where Abraham, the father of the Jewish nation, lived (Genesis 14:1-10). Lot, Abraham's nephew, was taken prisoner in battle.

> [13]Then a fugitive came and told Abram the Hebrew. Now he was living by the oaks of Mamre the Amorite, brother of Eshcol and brother of Aner, and these were allies with Abram. [14]and when Abram heard that his relative had been taken captive, he led out his trained men, born in his house, three hundred and eighteen, and went in pursuit as far as Dan. [15]And he divided his forces against them by night, he and his servants, and defeated them, and pursued them as far as Hobah, which is north of Damascus. [16]And he brought back all the goods, and also brought back his relative Lot with his possessions, and also the women, and the people.

[17]Then after his return from the defeat of Chedorlaomer and the kings who were with him, the king of Sodom went out to meet him at the valley of Shaveh (that is, the King's Valley). [18]And Melchizedek king of Salem brought out bread and wine; now he was a priest of God Most High. [19]And he blessed him and said,

"Blessed be Abram of God Most High,
Possessor of heaven and earth;
[20]and blessed by God Most High,
Who has delivered your enemies into your hand."

and he gave him a tenth of all.
- Genesis 14:13-20

Abraham defeats the attackers and saves his nephew, Lot, and family. Melchizedek, one of the local kings, blesses Abraham and receives from him one tenth of the spoils taken in battle as tribute. Now, nothing is ever mentioned of Melchizedek's family, genealogy, work or death. He appears only here and not seen again. (Mentioned in Psalm 110:4 and Hebrews 7:1-ff). Briefly, this is what we know about him:

- He was king of Salem (Jerusalem).

- He used the same word for God that Abraham used: God Most High (Jehovah).

- He is referred to as a "Priest of God Most High" by Moses, the writer of Genesis.

- He takes the initiative to bless Abraham, and Abraham receives the blessing.

- He spoke the Word (prophesied).

- He received tithes from Abraham.

It is important to remember that all of this was done long before (400-500 years) Moses had given the Law to the Jews and instituted the sacrificial system.

Melchizedek and Jesus — Hebrews 7:1-10

The author here reviews who Melchizedek was in relationship to Christ.

> [1] For this Melchizedek, king of Salem, priest of the Most High God, who met Abraham as he was returning from the slaughter of the kings and blessed him, [2] to whom also Abraham apportioned a tenth part of all the spoils, was first of all, by the translation of his name, king of righteousness, and then also king of Salem, which is king of peace. [3] Without father, without mother, without genealogy, having neither beginning of days nor end of life, but made like the Son of God, he remains a priest perpetually.

He provides a brief review of events from Genesis 14:18-20. He gives the meaning of Melchizedek's name (my king is righteous). Salem is Jerusalem geographically but the word means "peace." The author focuses on the fact that nothing of his genealogy is mentioned and emphasizes that this is significant. He is suggesting, with these opening statements, that Melchizedek was a "type" or preview of the Messiah-King that would ultimately come. This is demonstrated by:

- His name - my king is righteous
- His position - both king and priest
- His work - the blessing of Abraham
- His genealogy - endless, no mention of father, no death recorded

Melchizedek was a preview of Jesus, in that he appeared in history as a type that would embody the qualities possessed by the Messiah when He would finally appear. He was a model to demonstrate what to look for when the real thing appeared.

> [4] Now observe how great this man was to whom Abraham, the patriarch, gave a tenth of the choicest spoils. [5] And those indeed of the sons of Levi who receive the priest's office have commandment in the Law to collect a tenth from the people, that is, from their brethren, although these are descended from Abraham. [6] But the one whose genealogy is not traced from them collected a tenth from Abraham and blessed the one who had the promises. [7] But without any dispute the lesser is blessed by the greater. [8] In this case mortal men receive tithes, but in that case one receives them, of whom it is witnessed that he lives on. [9] And, so to speak, through Abraham even Levi, who received tithes, paid tithes, [10] for he was still in the loins of his father when Melchizedek met him.

He demonstrates Melchizedek's greatness in comparison to Levi (the source of the priestly line) by showing that:

1. The greater gives the blessings and receives the tithes.

2. As the patriarch through whom the Levitical priesthood came, Abraham was the father of all the Aaronic priests.

3. In their meeting it was Abraham who paid tithes to Melchizedek and, in a way, so did all of his descendants, including Aaron and the Levitical priests after him.

When comparing the Levitical priesthood to Melchizedek we see:

- Melchizedek blessed the father of the Levites, the one who had the promises. The significance of this was that the superior individual was the one who offered the blessing, and the inferior (because of age or position) received the blessing.

- Melchizedek received tithes from Abraham who gave voluntarily (not like his descendants, the Levites, who collected the tithes as a requirement of the Law). The significance of this was that Melchizedek's greatness and position was not derived from the Law and was recognized by Abraham, the father of those who gave and administered the Law.

- Melchizedek's priesthood was of an eternal nature. As a man, he died, but by not recording his genealogy or death, Scripture symbolized that his ministry was of an eternal nature. The Levitical priesthood, on the other hand, kept careful genealogical records. This demonstrated that theirs was a temporary ministry continually interrupted by death and succession from one generation to another.

The author is going to great lengths to show that there are two types of priesthood.

1. One, embodied by Aaron, that served the Jews throughout the Old Testament period preparing them for the arrival of the Messiah. It was temporary, earthly and under Law.

2. The other, embodied by Melchizedek, served as a type pointing to Christ. It was eternal, heavenly, righteous and not under Law.

The conclusion was that the priesthood previewed by Melchizedek was greater. He summarizes his case:

> [11] Now if perfection was through the Levitical priesthood (for on the basis of it the people received the Law), what further need was there for another priest to arise according to the order of Melchizedek, and not be designated according to the order of Aaron? [12] For when the priesthood is changed, of necessity there takes place a change of law also.

If perfection (salvation, a true relationship with God, a clear conscience) could be achieved through the Levitical sacrificial priestly system (and the Law upon which it was based), then there was no need to change. On the other hand, if perfection was not through Aaron, then a change to another type of priest and system was needed (because if the Aaronic line goes, so does the system of Law upon which it is based).

> [13] For the one concerning whom these things are spoken belongs to another tribe, from which no one has officiated at the altar. [14] For it is evident that our Lord was descended from Judah, a tribe with reference to which Moses spoke nothing concerning priests.

He admits that as far as Jesus is concerned, He could have never served as a Jewish high priest since the Law clearly taught that only the descendants of Levi could serve in this capacity, and Jesus was descended from the tribe of Judah.

> [15] And this is clearer still, if another priest arises according to the likeness of Melchizedek, [16] who has become such not on the basis of a law of physical

> requirement, but according to the power of an indestructible life. [17] For it is attested of Him,
> "You are a priest forever
> According to the order of Melchizedek."

The author shows that Jesus isn't trying to be an Aaronic priest, He is a priest after another type, the type embodied by Melchizedek, a type whose features were different than Aaron's priesthood. These differences were seen in its eternal nature. Not a priesthood that was earthly or perishable like Aaron's. He quotes Psalm 110 to show that Jesus' priesthood was based on the power of indestructible life, not Law as Aaron's was, and this feature was spoken of by David long before.

> [18] For, on the one hand, there is a setting aside of a former commandment because of its weakness and uselessness [19] (for the Law made nothing perfect), and on the other hand there is a bringing in of a better hope, through which we draw near to God.

The result of this change of priesthood from the Aaronic type to the Melchizedek type is that the basis of each is changed also; Aaron based on Law, Melchizedek based on the power of eternal life. The result is that there will be a different outcome.

The Law (and its priesthood) could not resurrect men, clear consciences or draw men nearer to God. It could only remind them of sin and death. However, Jesus could accomplish all of these and thus He, as our High Priest, replaced the Law of sin and death as the basis for priesthood with the power of life and freedom as the basis for priesthood, clearly demonstrated by His miraculous ministry and resurrection.

²⁰ And inasmuch as it was not without an oath ²¹ (for they indeed became priests without an oath, but He with an oath through the One who said to Him,
"The Lord has sworn
And will not change His mind,
'You are a priest forever'");

²² so much the more also Jesus has become the guarantee of a better covenant.

In addition to this power, His followers have the guarantee of salvation because God has sworn that Jesus will accomplish all of this as High Priest forever. Old Testament high priests did not have God or themselves taking any oaths, but Jesus is in His place as High Priest based on divine power and an oath from God.

²³ The former priests, on the one hand, existed in greater numbers because they were prevented by death from continuing, ²⁴ but Jesus, on the other hand, because He continues forever, holds His priesthood permanently. ²⁵ Therefore He is able also to save forever those who draw near to God through Him, since He always lives to make intercession for them.

The important feature of Jesus' eternal priesthood is that He is always and will always be there to make intercession for those who believe in Him and come to God through Him. The Levitical priesthood had highs and lows. It was scattered during times of persecution. It suffered lapses in commitment and service caused by sinfulness, but the priesthood of Christ is steadily interceding for the saints every day - forever. It is the reason why sinful men can have eternal life. Eternal life is now possible because an eternal priest intercedes eternally for them (something the Levitical priesthood could not do and never claimed to do).

The writer makes a final comparison and review of the facts with a hook or bridge to the next section.

> [26] For it was fitting for us to have such a high priest, holy, innocent, undefiled, separated from sinners and exalted above the heavens;

When comparing the two it becomes evident that Jesus is exactly the kind of high priest that we (they) needed.

- Holy - separate unto God
- Innocent
- Undefiled
- Separate from sinners
- Exalted - with God in heaven

This is the kind of high priest we really need to act on our behalf, and Jesus is like this.

> [27] who does not need daily, like those high priests, to offer up sacrifices, first for His own sins and then for the sins of the people, because this He did once for all when He offered up Himself.

Here he introduces the idea that Christ offered Himself as sacrifice (hook to next section). Sinful men offered countless dead animals as sacrifice for sin, but our High Priest offered His own perfect life once, for all time, to atone for all sin. The important point here is that this was possible because Jesus did not have to offer sacrifice for His own sins first as the Levitical priests did. He had only one life and because it was sinless, He could offer it for others; because it was eternal, it covered sins from the beginning to the end of time.

> [28] For the Law appoints men as high priests who are weak, but the word of the oath, which came after the Law, appoints a Son, made perfect forever.

A final comment on the difference between the two. The Law (given by Moses) established the Aaronic priesthood and sacrificial system. It was temporary, and not meant to save but to remind and prepare. It was served by weak and sinful men. God's Word, confirmed by an oath, later revealed the priesthood of Christ, as seen in Melchizedek, spoken of by David and fulfilled by Jesus. The author's unspoken conclusion asks his readers, "Do you really want to abandon this effective, eternal high priest for the former sinful and temporal ones?"

Summary

The author gives details concerning Melchizedek who was a type or model for the kind of high priest needed by men to complete their salvation, and he demonstrates how Jesus fulfills this type (righteous - without sin / eternal - without death).

He introduces two new ideas and changes:

1. If the priesthood changes, so does its base. Aaronic priesthood based on Law - Melchizedek priesthood based on the power of life.

2. The nature of the sacrifice. Aaronic priesthood offered animals and produce - Melchizedek priesthood offered the life of the high priest.

These ideas are introduced to form a bridge to the next section where the actual system of law and sacrifice will be examined.

This exhortation was meant to encourage these Jewish Christians to continue trusting in Jesus for salvation because He was a better high priest than Aaron. None of us today are in danger of returning to the Aaronic priesthood for salvation, so how does this encouragement apply to us? The issue we share with these first century Christians is the sense of sin and the fear of judgment we often experience. They were tempted to find someone else to guarantee their salvation. We also have our periods of doubt and fear. The message of Hebrews is clear, even for the modern reader, Jesus is always there for you!

> [25] Therefore He is able also to save forever those who draw near to God through Him, since He always lives to make intercession for them.

Don't ever let sin and failure of any kind discourage you because Jesus always intercedes on your behalf with the Father.

CHAPTER 8
JESUS: GREATER THAN THE JEWISH RELIGION
PART 1

Hebrews 8

In the previous chapter we finished the section in the letter to the Hebrews that explained Jesus' superiority as high priest over Aaron.

- Aaron and descendants as high priests - appointed by the Law, temporary and serviced by sinful men.

- Jesus as high priest - appointed by God, eternal in nature (Melchizedek type), serviced by a perfectly righteous divine being.

The point was that Jesus was a better and more effective high priest and they should not abandon Him for the lessor of the two.

The final section in part one of this epistle, chapter 8:10-18, will deal with His ministry. In other words, the author reviews Jesus' work as high priest, not only His credentials. He will say that:

- Where He works is superior (the sanctuary in heaven).

- The authority by which He works is superior (a new covenant based on better provisions).

- He will demonstrate that His work is superior (He offers a better sacrifice).

Chapter 8 serves as a bridge between the discussion on credentials and ministry as it introduces the two key ideas.

Jesus' Ministry is Superior to Aaron's Ministry

He has just demonstrated that Jesus is a more qualified high priest than Aaron. Now he will explain why Jesus' ministry is superior as well.

He Ministers in a Better Place — Hebrews 8:1-15

> [1] Now the main point in what has been said is this: we have such a high priest, who has taken His seat at the right hand of the throne of the Majesty in the heavens, [2] a minister in the sanctuary and in the true tabernacle, which the Lord pitched, not man.

"Now the main point..." refers to what the author is about to say. It is the climax of what he has explained previously. This

Jesus, once having offered His sacrifice, is not like the earthly priests who continually offer sacrifice; who do so in a man-made place; who have no rest. This Jesus sits (denoting authority, completeness) at the right hand of God; He is the minister (priest) that serves the true (real, eternal) sanctuary where God dwells (heaven). The true sanctuary is the one where God actually resides so the place where Jesus ministers is superior.

> [3] For every high priest is appointed to offer both gifts and sacrifices; so it is necessary that this high priest also have something to offer.

He reintroduces the idea of Jesus' sacrifice (offering), but doesn't develop the thought yet. He merely states the fact that just as the Levitical priests had sacrifices to work with in their daily ritual offerings, Jesus as a priest also needs to have a sacrifice to offer. He has already said that Jesus' sacrifice was Himself, but in repeating this he prepares his readers for another discussion on this point later on.

> [4]Now if He were on earth, He would not be a priest at all, since there are those who offer the gifts according to the Law; [5] who serve a copy and shadow of the heavenly things, just as Moses was warned by God when he was about to erect the tabernacle; for, "See," He says, "that you make all things according to the pattern which was shown you on the mountain."

The issue here is that the Levitical priests offered their sacrifices in an earthly setting given to them by Moses according to God's plan. The tabernacle in the desert was only a copy of the true and eternal sanctuary that already existed in heaven (Exodus 25:40). Moses had to be careful to follow the instructions given to him by God in constructing it.

- The tabernacle had two compartments and very few furnishings. It was where the priests did their work in offering sacrifices.

- While in the desert it was assembled and disassembled by the Levites, and the Israelite tribes camped around it, each in their specific location so that the tabernacle was located in the center of the camp.

- God's presence was marked by pillar of smoke in the day and a pillar of fire at night.

- Its construction and furnishings were designed by God and it was the model for the temple that would later be built by Solomon in Jerusalem.

The author was showing them the different locations where the ministry of the old high priest and the new high priest took place. The priests after Aaron were imperfect and temporal, and they served in a copy or shadow of the true sanctuary where Christ, the righteous and eternal high priest serves, which is in heaven.

He Ministers According to a Better Covenant — Hebrews 8:6-13

The author adds another argument to his presentation of the idea that Jesus' ministry is superior to Aaron's, not only does Jesus minister in a better place, but He does so by the authority of a better covenant which He mediates.

The word "covenant" means agreement, but God's covenants with men were promises which He bound Himself to keep. The word does not mean "a contract" in the business sense;

these contracts are usually negotiated by two parties each contributing ideas, requests, etc., and then ratified by an agreement once everyone is satisfied.

God, on the other hand, used covenants (promises) to progressively reveal His ultimate plan of saving man and granting him eternal life in heaven. Because of sin, men were slow to understand God's will and way, therefore God slowly revealed what He was doing through a series of promises or covenants. For example:

- **Noah** (Genesis 9:9-17) - Covenant/promise not to destroy the earth again with a flood and to guarantee the seasons despite man's failures.

- **Abraham** (Genesis 17:1-8) - Covenant/promise to give him a special land and bless the world through his descendants.

- **Moses** (Exodus 6:7) - Covenant/promise to make the Jews His special people and to bless them in particular.

These covenants had special features that made them different than what we refer to as "contracts":

1. God conceived and established all the details within the covenant, not man. Man had no input.

2. The covenant included all to whom it spoke. For example, Noah's covenant spoke to the whole human race; Abraham's, to his descendants only; Mosaic, to the Jewish nation.

3. God's covenants could not be changed by man. Man could, by his choosing, not benefit from the covenant, but he couldn't change the terms or prevent it from being fulfilled. For example, Noah could have refused to build the ark and drowned; Abraham could have

refused circumcision as the sign of God's promise and remained a nomad without descendants or land; Moses could have disobeyed God's laws and separated himself from the nation.

The author is saying here that God has made a new covenant/promise with man with better conditions which reveal His final purpose (the other covenants were designed to prepare man for this final one). This new covenant had another mediator, not Noah, Abraham or Moses, but Jesus Christ (a basic argument from a Christian viewpoint in rejecting the claims of the Islamic religion is the idea that God has not made a new covenant with Mohammed to replace the one He made through Jesus).

The word "mediator" would have been familiar to the readers of this letter. It meant arbitrator, someone to help bring two parties together. One who "stood in the middle." Jesus was the ideal representative for both God and man, the two parties included in this covenant. He not only revealed its details to man (through the preaching of the gospel) but also fulfilled its conditions for both God and man. As mediator, Jesus offered Himself as a perfect sacrifice on behalf of men to God, and then gave man the Holy Spirit on behalf of God (Acts 2:36-38).

> [6] But now He has obtained a more excellent ministry, by as much as He is also the mediator of a better covenant, which has been enacted on better promises.

His ministry is better because the covenant upon which it is based is better. This better covenant has been enacted (put into operation) because it is based on better promises (ones which reveal the fulfillment of God's purpose which is to save man and give all believers in Jesus eternal life). No other religion offers better promises.

> [7] For if that first covenant had been faultless, there would have been no occasion sought for a second.

The author confirms his statement by pointing to a self-evident fact: there would be no need for the new if the old one had succeeded (they knew it hadn't and so they could not argue with this reasoning). This did not mean that God had failed, it simply meant that His intentions were not completed with the old covenant.

> [8] For finding fault with them, He says,
> "Behold, days are coming, says the Lord,
> When I will effect a new covenant
> With the house of Israel and with the house of Judah;
> [9] Not like the covenant which I made with their fathers
> On the day when I took them by the hand
> To lead them out of the land of Egypt;
> For they did not continue in My covenant,
> And I did not care for them, says the Lord.

He quotes Jeremiah 31:31-ff, an Old Testament prophet, to show that even six centuries before Christ the setting aside of the covenant with the Jews would be necessary, not because God could not fulfill its promises (to bless them), but because they could not live within the conditions of the covenant given to them by God. The prophet says that a new covenant would be given, a different type was necessary, and the author of Hebrews is saying that this covenant has now been enacted by Jesus Christ. For Jewish Christians of that time this was the proof text from the Bible that they needed to accept this idea.

Conditions of the New Covenant

In the final section we see that this new covenant has three important features.

> [10]"For this is the covenant that I will make with the house of Israel
> After those days, says the Lord:
> I will put My laws into their minds,
> And I will write them on their hearts.
> And I will be their God,
> And they shall be My people.

1. The new covenant is inward focused and spiritual in nature

The Old Testament had the externals of ritual and God's commandments exposed on stone for all to see, learn and be measured by (the basic purpose of the Law - Romans 3:20). The rituals and architecture of the place of worship showed them that they could not come near to God. The Law revealed to them why this was so, they were not worthy.

With the new covenant, men would know God's laws, would have the willingness, hunger and thirst to do His will because they would have a sense of Him from within themselves. Not an outward sense, through religious rites, but inwardly through intimate knowledge. It was akin to what Jesus referred to as being "born again" (John 3:3-6). This inward transformation would be accomplished by the Word as revealed by Christ, and the transforming power of the Holy Spirit given at baptism (Acts 2:38).

> [11] "And they shall not teach everyone his fellow citizen,
> And everyone his brother, saying, 'Know the Lord,'

For all will know Me,
From the least to the greatest of them.

2. The new covenant is both personal and universal

Before, only the scribes and rulers could teach. They were the experts and with them resided the knowledge of God. In the new covenant, divine matters would not be the private possession of a particular class (priest, scribe). With the new covenant the promise was made that there would be personal, intimate knowledge of God and that everyone (rich, poor, educated or not) would have access to the knowledge of God, not just His law, but Himself!

[12] "For I will be merciful to their iniquities,
And I will remember their sins no more."

3. The new covenant deals effectively with sin

In the old covenant sacrifice was offered in order to remind the people of sin. The conscience could never be clear because the sacrificing served as a continual reminder of sin. In the new covenant there is a forgetting of sin (made possible by Christ's once for all sacrifice) thus freeing the conscience and purifying the heart. We will see later that this forgiveness of sins is the action upon which all the blessings and promises are based.

[13] When He said, "A new covenant," He has made the first obsolete. But whatever is becoming obsolete and growing old is ready to disappear.

The author goes back to Jeremiah's statement, 600 years before Christ, in referring to the new covenant He would make. The point being that the writing was already on the wall for this covenant six centuries before, so to say that it was over was not an exaggeration in light of Jeremiah's prophecy. The prophet said that the old covenant would one day be removed and with the arrival of Jesus, the new one appeared.

Summary

The lesson here for us and every generation is that those who receive forgiveness of sins (and all have access to this through Christ) will be changed, born again, become new creations from the inside out! We need not be discouraged when this doesn't happen all at once or is not steady. Instead, we should remember that the change in us through Christ is based on God's covenant, not our ability or our will power!

As long as we remain within the covenant by trust and obedience to Christ, God will change our hearts, come into closer union with us, and keep our conscious clear and ready for judgment day. These are the conditions that He has made and promised to fulfill in His covenant with each of us who believe in Jesus Christ.

CHAPTER 9

JESUS: GREATER THAN THE JEWISH RELIGION
PART 2

Hebrews 9

In his letter to Jewish Christians, the Hebrew writer is trying to encourage these brethren to remain faithful to Christ and not return to their former religion. He does this by demonstrating how Jesus is superior to every element of that faith. In the last section we looked at he explained that Jesus was not only superior to Aaron, the original high priest of Judaism, but that His ministry to the people was superior as well. For example:

- Jesus ministers in heaven (the true sanctuary) while they ministered on earth.

- He ministers according to a new covenant (promise) which has better features: it would be inward and spiritual (individual hearts would be changed) not just outward religious practice; it would be personal and universal (everyone would have access to God) not just the special ministers like priests and Levites; it would deal effectively with sin (not a covenant to help remember sin, but one to free people from the guilt of sin forever).

In the final chapter and a half of this first part of his letter, the author will continue building on this theme (the superiority of Jesus' ministry) by establishing two final ideas:

1. Jesus' work (ministry/sacrifice) is done in a better place, by a better covenant and is thus superior.

2. The results of Jesus' ministry on our behalf are superior than the results of the ministry performed by the Aaronic priests on behalf of the Jewish people.

These two ideas are not presented one after another but are intertwined throughout this section.

The Tabernacle Ritual — Hebrews 9:1-5

The author begins by reviewing the worship elements in the "Tabernacle" serviced by the Old Testament priests during the Jewish people's wanderings in the desert.

[1] Now even the first covenant had regulations of divine worship and the earthly sanctuary. [2] For there was a tabernacle prepared, the outer one, in which were the lampstand and the table and the sacred bread; this is called the holy place. [3] Behind the second veil there was a tabernacle which is called the Holy of Holies, [4] having a golden altar of incense and the ark of the covenant covered on all sides with gold, in which was a golden jar holding the manna, and Aaron's rod which budded, and the tables of the

covenant; [5] and above it were the cherubim of glory overshadowing the mercy seat; but of these things we cannot now speak in detail.

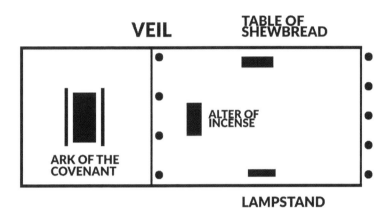

VEIL

TABLE OF SHEWBREAD

ALTER OF INCENSE

ARK OF THE COVENANT

LAMPSTAND

The only source of light inside the two-room tabernacle was a lampstand situated against the southern wall. The showbread, located on the northern wall, was always set before the Lord. There were twelve loaves (one per tribe) baked fresh every Sabbath. The old loaves were eaten by the priests.

The Holy of Holies was a smaller inner room that had only two pieces of furniture: an altar of incense which may have been placed directly in front of the veil in the outer compartment so that the smoke of the burning incense entered into the Holy of Holies when burned there, and the Ark of the Covenant which was a box covered in gold measuring four and a half feet long and two and a half feet wide as well as high. It contained Aaron's rod (which had miraculously budded) and a jar of manna, both of which were lost with time. It also contained the tablets inscribed with the Ten Commandments. These were still in the ark when Solomon built the temple in Jerusalem (I Kings 8:9) several hundred years later.

The Ark was covered by a lid decorated with two angels facing each other. This was called the "mercy-seat" because it was here that the high priest sprinkled the blood of sacrifice on the Day of Atonement. This was done once per year and signified a temporary (needed to be done each year) reconciliation between God and His people.

The Work of the Priests — Hebrews 9:6-10

> [6] Now when these things have been so prepared, the priests are continually entering the outer tabernacle performing the divine worship, [7] but into the second, only the high priest enters once a year, not without taking blood, which he offers for himself and for the sins of the people committed in ignorance. [8] The Holy Spirit is signifying this, that the way into the holy place has not yet been disclosed while the outer tabernacle is still standing, [9] which is a symbol for the present time. Accordingly both gifts and sacrifices are offered which cannot make the worshiper perfect in conscience, [10] since they relate only to food and drink and various washings, regulations for the body imposed until a time of reformation.

At this point the author goes on to describe the type of work and ministry that the high priests did in these surroundings. The priests went into the outer compartment every day to trim the lamp (morning and evening), offer incense (morning and evening) and replace the showbread each Sabbath day. In addition to these duties there was the daily offering of sacrifices using animals, produce, oil and wine etc. Once per year (Day of Atonement), however, the high priest would enter the inner sanctuary (Holy of Holies). He would first offer incense and then offer the blood of a sacrificed animal for his own sins. Only after this was done would he offer the blood of another sacrifice for the sins of the people.

N

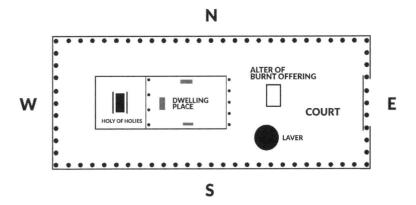

W   **E**

S

The author says that the significance of this type of ministry was to demonstrate that man could not come near to God. It was a continual testimony through ritual that the way to God was blocked. The tabernacle's design and restricted access represented how separated the people were from God.

The complex external rituals had the ability to remove ceremonial uncleanliness (i.e. if a Jew became unclean ceremonially he could not participate in corporate worship or social interaction - becoming "clean" again required the offering of a sacrifice and a series of other rituals - Leviticus 5:1-5; 16:16-22; 21:18-21), but they could not clean the conscience. This type of cleansing, the author said, would only be done at the time of "reformation." Reformation was a reference to the coming of the Messiah, Jesus.

Jesus' Ministry Described
— Hebrews 9:11-22

At this point the writer moves forward to describe Jesus' ministry as High Priest.

The Effectiveness of His Sacrifice

> [11] But when Christ appeared as a high priest of the good things to come, He entered through the greater and more perfect tabernacle, not made with hands, that is to say, not of this creation; [12] and not through the blood of goats and calves, but through His own blood, He entered the holy place once for all, having obtained eternal redemption.

Jesus ministers in the same way as the other high priests, by offering sacrifice for sin, however:

1. He offers sacrifice in the heavenly sanctuary, not the earthly one.

2. He offers His own perfect, eternal life for the sins of men, not that of dead animals.

3. He makes a more valuable payment (perfect, eternal sacrifice) and thus obtains a more valuable outcome (eternal redemption), not just ceremonial cleansing or an annual reprieve for sin.

> [13] For if the blood of goats and bulls and the ashes of a heifer sprinkling those who have been defiled, sanctify for the cleansing of the flesh, [14] how much more will the blood of Christ, who through the eternal Spirit offered Himself without blemish to God,

cleanse your conscience from dead works to serve the living God?

Here the author compares the two sacrifices in a positive way. He agrees that according to the Law, animal sacrifice was effective to render acceptable before God those who had violated some aspects of the external rituals of their religion. For example, one who had come into contact with a corpse was considered unclean and not allowed to participate in collective religious activity. However, if a purification rite was performed with the blood of an animal, this person was restored to the fellowship of his brothers. The point was this: if the blood (life) of an animal would accomplish this, imagine what the sacrifice of the Son of God could do? It would not simply remove a charge for breaking ceremonial law, but also the guilt and fear resulting from breaking God's eternal spiritual laws. The implication was that once cleansed by this sacrifice, the individual was free from condemnation, guilt and fear, and free to serve God with a spirit of enthusiasm, not one of slavery. Here is where the sacrifice of Christ proved its effectiveness: in the change that it created in the heart of a sinner.

The Reason for His Sacrifice

The author has made the case for Jesus' superior ministry by demonstrating that where He ministers (heaven) and what He does in ministering (redeems/saves) is far better than what the ministry of the Jewish priests accomplished; and this should be the climax of his argument. However, he has one more point to make for his readers because they are Jews, and that is to answer the question, "Why did Jesus have to die?" For Jews, the death of the Messiah was a great obstacle to faith in Jesus. If He was the Messiah promised in Scripture, why should He have to die? After all, they reasoned, "He came to save the people, not to be killed

Himself." In answer to this question, the author gives two reasons for Jesus' death on the cross:

> [15] And for this reason He is the mediator of a new covenant, in order that since a death has taken place for the redemption of the transgressions that were committed under the first covenant, those who have been called may receive the promise of the eternal inheritance.

1. A sacrifice for sin requires death. This is an unbreakable spiritual law very much like "gravity" is a physical law. The penalty for sin is death, and in order to redeem (buy back) men's souls, Jesus had to pay with His life. Now, the fact that He was a divine (eternal) being as well as a human being meant that the sacrifice of His life purchased not only the forgiveness of sins on the day it was offered (like animals), but also obtained forgiveness for all time. The eternal nature of His life produced a sacrifice for sin that was eternal in nature as well. This is why, in explaining the power of Jesus' cross, many say that it goes back in time to the beginning in order to forgive the sins of Adam, and also forward to the end of time forgiving the sins of the last man alive when He will return at the end of the world. This is the first reason why Jesus is the mediator (go between) of the new covenant (promise) that God has with man - only Jesus has a perfect, eternal life to offer in order to accomplish this forgiveness for all men and for all time. He offers a one-time sacrifice. This sacrifice is what pays for our forgiveness and the eternal life that this forgiveness permits. These blessings are referred to as an "inheritance" reserved for those who are called. The author uses two meanings for this word: Covenant - a promise to do something; Will - a testament or will after one's death. We are called by

the gospel to come and obtain our inheritance prepared by God and paid for by the sacrifice of Jesus.

2. This bring us to the second reason for His death. In order for a will to be executed and the people to receive their "inheritance" there needs to be the death of the principal party. In verses 16-21 the Hebrew writer says that it was necessary for Jesus to die because without His death, the will or testament that grants us our inheritance would not come into effect.

[16]For where a covenant is, there must of necessity be the death of the one who made it. [17]For a covenant is valid only when men are dead, for it is never in force while the one who made it lives. [18]Therefore even the first covenant was not inaugurated without blood. [19]For when every commandment had been spoken by Moses to all the people according to the Law, he took the blood of the calves and the goats, with water and scarlet wool and hyssop, and sprinkled both the book itself and all the people, [20]saying, "THIS IS THE BLOOD OF THE COVENANT WHICH GOD COMMANDED YOU." [21]And in the same way he sprinkled both the tabernacle and all the vessels of the ministry with the blood.

He demonstrates that even the first covenant (Old Testament) was put into effect when animal sacrifices were made and the actual external elements of the Jewish faith (tablets, tables, sanctuary, etc.) were sprinkled with its blood (Exodus 40:9-15; Leviticus 8). So too with the new covenant. He summarizes his argument by saying that there is no cleansing or forgiving without the shedding of blood (offering of life). In the Old Testament they did it with animals; now, Jesus had done it also with His own life, this is why He had to die. He was the Messiah, but God's plan was that the Savior would save by offering His life as sacrifice.

The Superiority of His Sacrifice — Hebrews 9:23-28

> [23] Therefore it was necessary for the copies of the things in the heavens to be cleansed with these, but the heavenly things themselves with better sacrifices than these. For Christ did not enter a holy place made with hands, a mere copy of the true one, but into heaven itself, now to appear in the presence of God for us;

The tabernacle and religious objects were purified with an animal sacrifice. However, Jesus who entered the true tabernacle (where God is in heaven), needed to come with a better sacrifice. The earthly temple demanded earthly sacrifices and the heavenly temple required a sacrifice of a spiritual nature like Christ's.

> [25] nor was it that He should offer Himself often, as the high priest enters the holy place year by year with blood not his own. [26] Otherwise, He would have needed to suffer often since the foundation of the world; but now once at the consummation of the ages He has been manifested to put away sin by the sacrifice of Himself.

The priests offered numerous sacrifices of animals given to them by the people over the centuries, but now, at the appointed time, Christ has offered Himself, done once for all time. Jesus does not repeatedly go in and out of the temple to do His priestly duties. His service is done one time and He remains in the sanctuary to prepare a place within it for those who follow Him, things that the Jewish priests could not and were never called upon to do.

> [27] And inasmuch as it is appointed for men to die once and after this comes judgment, [28]so Christ also, having been offered once to bear the sins of many, shall appear a second time for salvation without reference to sin, to those who eagerly await Him.

All men die once (according to God's plan) and then are judged. Jesus, as a man, also died only once, but His death was not on account of sin (Romans 6:23). His death was as a sacrifice for sin. All men will return to be judged after their death. Jesus, as God's Son, will also return, but not in connection with sin (this He dealt with at the cross). When He returns next time it will be to gather those who have faithfully followed Him, and bring these to heaven to be with God eternally.

Summary

1. In this section the writer of Hebrews compares Jesus' work/ministry with that of the Old Testament priests: Jesus offers His sacrifice in heaven, they on earth; His sacrifice is eternal, theirs temporal; His sacrifice removes the guilt of sin, theirs only ritual impurity, and as a reminder of sin.

2. The author also gives two reasons why the Messiah had to die: sin is paid for by offering a sacrifice, and sacrifice can only be offered through death, thus Jesus' sacrifice of Himself required His death; and the promises contained in the covenant/will/inheritance

prepared by God for us required a death in order to put it into effect.

3. He summarizes Jesus' superior ministry: He offers a better sacrifice in a better place; He offers a one-time sacrifice for all sin; and He will return, not to be judged like the Jewish priests (as humans), but (as the Messiah) to gather the saved to heaven.

There is no other religion where God reveals such a clear plan of salvation in a historical context. God's actions and purposes are seen from the beginning (creation), to the completion of His will (the cross and resurrection), to a preview of the end of time (Jesus' return for judgment and reward). And, no other religion reveals our role as believers so clearly as well: believe and remain faithful to Christ to the end.

We need to remember that our lives are not about cars or computers, health, taxes, even homes and families. Our lives are about faith and how faith works itself out against the backdrop of these other things. The "big" picture is always about us being faithful in good or bad times. The Hebrew writer is trying to give his readers the support they need in order to keep the bigger picture in focus by regaining the faith that they were losing.

CHAPTER 10
JESUS: GREATER THAN THE JEWISH RELIGION
PART 3

Hebrews 10:1-8

In the book of Hebrews, the author is showing Christ's superiority over the entire system of religion as embodied by the Jewish priesthood and sacrificial rituals in the Old Testament. In this final section of the first part of the book he reviews the necessity of Jesus' sacrifice and its effectiveness in comparison to the sacrificial death of animals in the Old Testament. Before, the author argued that Jesus was a greater high priest than Aaron because of His qualifications (God's Son), the place where He ministered (heaven), and the type of sacrifice He offered (Himself). Now he will close his case by demonstrating that the results of Jesus' ministry on behalf of the people was also superior than the results of the Jewish high priest's ministry for the Jewish people. This is the climax of his letter. If the results are better, it is proof that everything else is true.

The Results of Jewish High Priest's Work — Hebrews 10:1-4

> [1] For the Law, since it has only a shadow of the good things to come and not the very form of things, can never by the same sacrifices year by year, which they offer continually, make perfect those who draw near. [2] Otherwise, would they not have ceased to be offered, because the worshipers, having once been cleansed, would no longer have had consciousness of sins?

He begins by arguing that if the sacrifices offered in the Old Testament worked, they would have cleansed the consciences the priests who offered them (by authority and command of the Law). The proof of this would be that the people would have stopped offering them since they would no longer feel guilty and would be confident of salvation. The author argues that the shadow (outline, rough sketch) can never be greater than the finished work or form, and that the Old Testament sacrifices were just the shadow but not the real thing. A million shadows cannot equal one real thing. The Old Testament sacrifices were merely the shadow of the sacrifice of Christ, the real thing.

> [3] But in those sacrifices there is a reminder of sins year by year. [4] For it is impossible for the blood of bulls and goats to take away sins.

The author repeats the idea that the sacrifices in the Old Testament were to serve as a reminder/remembrance of sin, not as the actual offering for sin, that was to come later (In comparison to the sacrificial rituals of the Old Testament we note that the ritual of the Lord's Supper is a remembrance of the sacrifice that does take away sin, not sin itself). In fact, he says, the blood (life) of animals could not remove sins, no matter how many were sacrificed, and explains why this was so in the next verse.

Christ's Sacrifice — verses 5-10

God has always known that animal sacrifice could not remove sin, but now the author answers why Jesus' sacrifice does.

> [5]Therefore, when He comes into the world, He says,
> "SACRIFICE AND OFFERING THOU HAST NOT DESIRED,
> BUT A BODY THOU HAST PREPARED FOR ME;
> [6]IN WHOLE BURNT OFFERINGS AND sacrifices FOR SIN THOU HAST TAKEN NO PLEASURE.
> [7]THEN I SAID, 'BEHOLD, I HAVE COME
> (IN THE ROLL OF THE BOOK IT IS WRITTEN OF ME)
> TO DO THY WILL, O GOD.'"

The author explains this by using Psalm 40:6-8 which, in the original context as it was written by David, sees David expressing a pledge to do God's will rather than offering formal sacrifices. David understood the essential truth about spiritual life, that obedience to God's will (as he had learned it from the Scriptures) was what God wanted and what sustained man's soul, not animal sacrifices or any sort of ritual for that matter.

> [8]After saying above, "SACRIFICES AND
> OFFERINGS AND WHOLE BURNT OFFERINGS
> AND sacrifices FOR SIN THOU HAST NOT
> DESIRED, NOR HAST THOU TAKEN PLEASURE in
> them" (which are offered according to the
> Law), [9]then He said, "BEHOLD, I HAVE COME TO
> DO THY WILL." He takes away the first in order to
> establish the second. [10]By this will we have been
> sanctified through the offering of the body of Jesus
> Christ once for all.

The author now takes this quote and this idea and applies
them to Jesus and His sacrifice. What makes Jesus' sacrifice
effective is that it involves the will of God. In verse 9 he says
that Jesus was willing to offer Himself. The point here is that
animals have no choice or will, therefore their value as
sacrifice is basically their earthly value as animals.

He goes on to say in verse 10 that it was God's will that a
perfect sacrifice be offered, and in doing so Jesus was doing
God's will. What gives life and obtains forgiveness is the
doing of God's will. The offering of Jesus' life would have
accomplished nothing had it not been in accordance with
God's will. Jesus knew God's will in what was needed to
remove the guilt as a result of man's sin, and did it. In so
doing, man's sins were removed forever.

Once God's will has been accomplished in this regard, there
is no need to repeat it. It is done once for all time. Now, even
if a mere human being knew that this was God's will, he could
not accomplish it because he lacked the perfect life and divine
nature required. On the other hand, Jesus, divine Son of God,
given a human body, knowing God's will and living a sinless
life was willing and, more importantly, *able* to do it.

Final Summary of Christ's Superiority — verses 11-18

The author makes a final comparison of the two kinds of priests: the Levitical priest and Jesus as priest.

> [11] And every priest stands daily ministering and offering time after time the same sacrifices, which can never take away sins;

He says that the Old Testament priest (still serving in this capacity at the time that the author wrote this letter) continued with his daily task of sacrificial offerings, and all for no results other than to remind one of sin (and since sin was ever present, the work was never ending).

> [12] but He, having offered one sacrifice for sins for all time, SAT DOWN AT THE RIGHT HAND OF GOD, [13] waiting from that time onward UNTIL HIS ENEMIES BE MADE A FOOTSTOOL FOR HIS FEET. [14] For by one offering He has perfected for all time those who are sanctified.

Jesus as high priest, however, offers His perfect sacrifice according to God's will in heaven, and only once. He then sits down at the right hand of God, never to offer the sacrifice again! His work is done and He sits at a place of exaltation, power and authority (unlike the Jewish priest whose work is never finished and accomplishes nothing in regards to salvation). Jesus has accomplished the purification of all men's souls thereby freeing them from guilt and condemnation. There is no need for any more sacrifices, His has accomplished God's will.

Note that in Matthew 27:50-51 where Jesus, on the cross, has breathed His last with the words, "It is finished...", Matthew records that at that moment the veil in the temple separating the holy place from the Holy of Holies was torn in two. This signified, among other things, that the need for sacrifice to approach God was over. The way to enter was now clear, and that way was through faith in Jesus Christ.

The author makes a final appeal to the Old Testament saying that this is what God promised all along. This is what He wanted, and the nature and results of Jesus' sacrifice shows that all of this was in accordance with the Scriptures.

> [15]And the Holy Spirit also bears witness to us; for after saying, [16]"THIS IS THE COVENANT THAT I WILL MAKE WITH THEM AFTER THOSE DAYS, SAYS THE LORD: I WILL PUT MY LAWS UPON THEIR HEART, AND UPON THEIR MIND I WILL WRITE THEM," He then says, [17]"AND THEIR SINS AND THEIR LAWLESS DEEDS I WILL REMEMBER NO MORE."

Verses 15-17 are a quote from Jeremiah 31:33-ff where the prophet is revealing what the ultimate end of God's work among His people will be: they will have a new covenant (better promise), they will have an intimate knowledge of Him and His will. In other words, they will be able to know God subjectively and not only objectively. They will know Him personally and not just know about Him. Their sins will be forgiven and forgotten, not just exposed before them year after year. Some ask, "Will we remember our sins in heaven?" According to Hebrews it seems that if God does not remember them, we won't either.

> ¹⁸ Now where there is forgiveness of these things, there is no longer any offering for sin.

The author finishes by stating that once forgiveness has appeared, it means that the old is gone and the promises spoken of by the prophets are now here.

Summary

In the last section of the first part of this epistle the author brings home the point that Jesus' work as high priest is superior to that of Aaron and his descendants.

1. He shows that Old Testament sacrifices never accomplished the cleansing of the conscience from guilt, no matter how many were offered.

2. He demonstrates that Christ's sacrifice was effective to remove guilt because it was offered according to God's will.

3. He summarizes his own arguments by comparing Jesus and the Levitical priests one last time. He does this by stating that they (Jewish priests) have an endless task that does not achieve true sanctification, but Jesus, as High Priest offering Himself as sacrifice, accomplishes God's will which was His own exaltation and our redemption.

The author's purpose was to compare the Levitical religious system and Jesus Christ to demonstrate Jesus' superiority as a person and as a minister for our spiritual needs. We had to learn a lot about the Jewish religion in order to make sure of what the author was saying as he compared the two. He will draw his final conclusions in the last few chapters.

This epistle demonstrates Christ's superiority (or one could correctly say, fulfillment) to the Jewish religion which was the most developed religious system of the time since it was given by God as a forerunner to Christianity. However, with the Bible as a whole, we can also demonstrate how Christ is superior to any religious system, past, present or future. Of course, the author wasn't talking about systems, he was talking about Jesus Christ, the resurrected Son of God, who is the ruler of the universe and will judge all men and their religions.

Please do not feel ashamed, afraid or embarrassed to claim that Christ is the only way to come to God. The author eloquently argued this case to the Jews 2000 years ago, but we can/must also make this case today to Muslims, Buddhists, Hindus and others who have not received what only Jesus can give them, and that is forgiveness of sins. No other religion offers this, but all need it.

CHAPTER 11

THE CHURCH OF CHRIST ENDURES

Hebrews 10:19-39

At this point of his letter the author will bring the lesson home to his readers. In the previous sections he has warned them about falling back and the terrible consequences for one who, after having known the Lord, abandons Him. Now, he exhorts them in a positive way by pointing out what they ought to be doing.

If Jesus is superior to the Jewish faith and its system, then His people, the church, are glorious as well. He tells them that as the church of the glorious Christ they must also be glorious. He will further explain that the two main ways that they can glorify Jesus are by being faithful and holy. In this chapter we will look at what he says about the glory of a faithful church.

The Glory of the Faithful Church — Hebrews 10:19-25

Previously, the author has explained that the Lord glorifies the church with all of His qualifications and service on its behalf. He will now show that the church returns that glory to its Lord through faithfulness to Him. This faithfulness, he will say, is expressed as confidence in Him.

> [19] Since therefore, brethren, we have confidence to enter the holy place by the blood of Jesus, [20]by a new and living way which He inaugurated for us through the veil, that is, His flesh.

Christ has opened a new way to come before God (His perfect and eternal sacrifice). The old way (dead animal sacrifices) did not give men access to the throne of God, it only reminded them of their estrangement, weakness, condemnation and death. The new way gives those who approach confidence, not fear; brings all into the very presence of God, not the outer court; provides life, and not death. If we have confidence because of Jesus and what He has done, what should this confidence move us to do? In the next few verses the author will name three things in particular:

1. Draw Near to God with Faith

> [21]and since we have a great priest over the house of God, [22]let us draw near with a sincere heart in full assurance of faith, having our hearts sprinkled clean from an evil conscience and our bodies washed with pure water.

Jesus is the priest that ministers for us so, unlike the Jews, Christians should draw near to God with a sincere heart free of fear, ignorance, guilt or sin because the Christian is free from the sins that cause these. Even the high priest could not enter the Holy of Holies this way because, even though he was clean ceremonially on the outside, his heart had not yet been cleansed by the blood of Christ. His water purification rites cleansed the outside, but the baptism of Jesus signaled the cleansing of the conscience (I Peter 3:21).

2. Hold Fast our Confession of Hope

> [23]Let us hold fast the confession of our hope without wavering, for He who promised is faithful;

The confession (their religious beliefs) is what gives them hope. He admonishes them not to doubt the reality of the promises made by God through Christ because God is faithful and able to fulfill His promises. The hope is that they would be resurrected and have eternal life. This hope was sure because it was based on God's promise, and they were not to doubt it (waver).

3. Consider One Another in Love

> [24]and let us consider how to stimulate one another to love and good deeds, [25]not forsaking our own assembling together, as is the habit of some, but encourage one another; and all the more, as you see the day drawing near.

While they approach God faithfully, secure in their hope, they are to encourage each other with and toward good deeds and all with a loving regard. Some had drawn back from God, given up hope and abandoned the faith. This was evident because they had stopped coming to the assemblies (a barometer of spiritual health). He tells them to encourage one another, not only to attend church services regularly, but to encourage one another while they were actually at church assemblies so that weak Christians would not become discouraged and leave the church. (If people are not encouraged by loving attention, teaching, help, etc. while they are in the assembly, all the encouragement to return to the assembly will not bring them back.) He adds that they should all do this, as they see the "day" coming near. The "day" mentioned here could be a reference to several things:

- Day = Lord's Day
- Day = Destruction of Jerusalem
- Day = Return of Jesus

The author was probably referring to the return of Jesus since his readers were located outside of Palestine and could not witness the warning signs of the eventual destruction of that city by the Roman army after a long siege in 70 AD (Matthew 24). This may not refer to the Lord's Day either because the author is discussing what they ought to be doing within the assembly and not merely having to attend. And so, Christians should be confident because Christ has prepared a new life-giving way for them to come to God, and this new confidence should spurn them to express this boldness by:

- Drawing near to God in faith (without fear)
- Being strong in their hope (without doubt)
- Encouraging others in love (without hesitation)

The Unfaithful will be Punished — Hebrews 10:26-31

The author encourages the faithful to boldly go forward, and not to retreat because retreating will have terrible consequences.

> [26]For if we go on sinning willfully after receiving the knowledge of the truth, there no longer remains a sacrifice for sins, [27]but a certain terrifying expectation of judgment, and THE FURY OF A FIRE WHICH WILL CONSUME THE ADVERSARIES.

There is a sacrifice for those who sin and need forgiveness, but there is no sacrifice for those who know the truth, and despite this, willfully continue to sin. The only things left for them, he says, are judgment and punishment. Of course, there is a difference between the individual acts of sin which all, including Christians, are guilty of from time to time.

The Hebrew writer is describing the state of sin where one knows that what he does is sinful and, without any attempt at repentance or help from God, continues willfully to practice it. In this discussion of sin the author includes the sin of abandoning the assembly because it is the outward sign of a willful falling away from the faith (one cannot be faithful to Jesus, the head, without being faithful to the church, the body of Christ). Abandoning the assembly is merely the outward sign of the serious sin of falling away from the faith.

The Hebrew writer makes one final comparison between Jesus and the Jewish religion.

> [28]Anyone who has set aside the Law of Moses dies without mercy on the testimony of two or three witnesses. [29]How much severer punishment do you think he will deserve who has trampled under foot the Son of God, and has regarded as unclean the blood of the covenant by which he was sanctified, and has insulted the spirit of grace? [30]For we know Him who said, "VENGEANCE IS MINE, I WILL REPAY." And again, "THE LORD WILL JUDGE HIS PEOPLE."

The author states that since Jesus is greater than the Jewish religion, the sin of abandoning Him is greater than the sin of abandoning the Jewish faith, and so will the punishment. According to Judaism, a sinner was found guilty and punished without mercy based on the testimony of two or three human witnesses. Under the new covenant one who abandons Christ has:

1. Held up to contempt God's own Son.
2. Considered His blood or sacrifice no better than any other.
3. Rejected the Holy Spirit.

Such sins were not even possible under the Law of Moses in the Old Testament period. This is why the author says that they are greater. The reasoning he makes is that if God punished men for lessor offenses, how much greater the punishment for one who is found guilty of such things, especially knowing that only a saved person could commit these sins.

> ³¹It is a terrifying thing to fall into the hands of the living God.

He concludes by saying that for the faithful child of God it is a wonderful and reassuring thing to be in the hands of God, but for the rebel, the one who knowingly rejects Christ, that same position is terrifying because God has absolute power to destroy him forever.

The Faithful Church Endures — Hebrews 10:32-39

After warning them of the terrible consequences of falling away, the author gently encourages them to carry on and endure.

> ³²But remember the former days, when, after being enlightened, you endured a great conflict of sufferings, ³³partly by being made a public spectacle through reproaches and tribulations, and partly by becoming sharers with those who were so treated. ³⁴For you showed sympathy to the prisoners, and accepted joyfully the seizure of your property, knowing that you have for yourselves a better possession and an abiding one.

The writer reminds them of their attitude of endurance demonstrated when they first came to the Lord. They were ridiculed publicly. They continued to associate with other believers who were also badly treated. They ministered to Christians who were jailed (an obligation that the first century church took seriously - Matthew 25:35-36). They suffered the loss of their own property because of their faith. Christianity was an outlawed religion and had no protection of the state, consequently during religious persecution many Christian homes were looted or lost altogether with no legal recourse. The author reminds them that they endured these things joyfully at the time because their hope for a better "home" was strong.

> 35Therefore, do not throw away your confidence, which has a great reward.

He tells them that he is aware that they faithfully endured these things at the beginning, and should not throw away their confidence now since the reward is still to come.

> 36For you have need of endurance, so that when you have done the will of God, you may receive what was promised.

They must continue until the end in the same way that they started so that they can receive the promises made to them at the beginning. They need endurance because doing God's will is not always easy, and often creates conflicts.

> 37FOR YET IN A VERY LITTLE WHILE,
> HE WHO IS COMING WILL COME, AND WILL NOT DELAY,
> 38BUT MY RIGHTEOUS ONE SHALL LIVE BY FAITH;
> AND IF HE SHRINKS BACK, MY SOUL HAS NO PLEASURE IN HIM.

He cites an Old Testament passage (Habakkuk 2:3-4) where the prophet was crying out to God asking why He allowed foreign oppressors to attack the Israelites. God's response was that no matter what happened He was still in charge, and that in time He would destroy the wicked. As for His people, they would survive and receive their reward if they remained faithful.

The author uses this passage as an encouragement to his readers who also had suffered persecution and discouragement. If they endured faithfully, God would rescue and reward them in the end as well. He also notes that God takes pleasure, not in the suffering of His people, but in their reaction to suffering (faithful endurance).

> [39]But we are not of those who shrink back to destruction, but of those who have faith to the preserving of the soul.

He summarizes his thoughts by saying that Christians are not quitters who go back to the old ways or to destruction, but forward by faith towards complete redemption and eternal life.

Summary

The author has shown how glorious Jesus is. Now, he shows how Jesus' church can be glorious by:

- Drawing near to God with confidence now that Jesus has opened the way by His sacrifice.

- Holding on to its hope without wavering, since this hope is built on God's promise.

- Providing loving encouragement to each other as they grow in Christian fellowship.

He warns the church that abandoning Christ is a greater sin than abandoning Moses because Christ is greater, and finally, he encourages them to finish the race with the same zeal that they began with so they can receive the rewards.

These Christians, as well as every disciple until the end of time, were learning some of the most basic lessons about the Christian life:

1. It is easy to begin in the Lord but hard to finish (Luke 14:25-34).

2. Every day you have to renew the decision that you will not allow anything to stop you from finishing the race (no person, sin, thing - Luke 14:26).

3. The rewards are only for those who finish (II Timothy 4:8).

In the Christian race it is not how fast you run, it is if you finish or not that's important. Many begin but few finish (Matthew 7:13).

CHAPTER 12

THE CHURCH OF CHRIST IS FAITHFUL

Hebrews 11

After having shown Christ's glory by demonstrating His superiority over the Jewish religion as its fulfillment, the author of the Hebrew letter goes on to exhort his readers to reflect that glory by being faithful to Him. He encourages them not to fall away as some have done, but because they have a great mediator in Christ, go forward in confidence, despite the obstacles they face. In chapter 11 he gives them a shortened version of their own history highlighting those individuals who, despite difficulty, continued to believe and serve God faithfully. He does this in order to show them two things:

1. That faith has always been the key response that God has desired from His people, not perfection, ceremony or eloquence.

2. That his readers are recipients of the blessings that all their predecessors were faithfully waiting for, but died before receiving.

> [1] Now faith is the assurance of things hoped for, the conviction of things not seen.

The first verse is more a description of faith than a definition. Faith, in Old Testament times, was seen as confidence in God, perseverance and a vision of the unseen. Faith, in the New Testament period, is more amply described and specific in definition. For example, New Testament faith requires that one believe as true the specific claims of Jesus Christ, and make a personal commitment to Him as Lord based on that faith (Mark 16:16). Sincere faith in the Christian era is clearly seen as the believer strives to obey Jesus' teachings (Luke 6:46; John 14:23), and follow Jesus, trusting in Him and His promises (John 14:2-3).

The author of the Hebrew letter says that faith is primarily two things:

1. Assurance - The original Greek word translated into the English word "assurance" referred to the substructure or the foundation of a building.

2. Conviction - The original Greek word translated into the English word "conviction" was a legal term referring to evidence upon which a case was built.

"Hope for things not seen" refers to the blessings and promises made by God through Christ (forgiveness, resurrection and eternal life). Based on the understanding of these words, the author is saying that faith, what it was in the Old Testament and fully realized in the New Testament, serves as a basis from which people gain the ability to stake their lives on unseen realities. It is the foundation that permits hope. The "yes to belief" that allows us to see the things that exist in the invisible or spiritual realm.

Comment

> [2] For by it the men of old gained approval.

In verse two the author makes one of four comments concerning faith in this passage. He states that it is by faith (confidence of things not seen) that men (their Jewish ancestors) gained approval from God. He reaffirms the point that this has always been the basis by which God approves of men, whether they have faith or not. This is not a new idea. He will go on to give numerous examples of people who were spoken well of by God on account of their faith.

1. Creation

> [3] By faith we understand that the worlds were prepared by the word of God, so that what is seen was not made out of things which are visible.

Before going on to specific people to confirm his statement he uses creation, the universal example of faith, as the basis for understanding. He says that we can only grasp the fact of creation by faith since it cannot be proven by scientific evidence or observation (we can deduce, but there are no witnesses). However, if we believe God's Word on the matter, the reason, nature and purpose for creation become clear to us.

138

2. Cain/Abel

> ⁴ By faith Abel offered to God a better sacrifice than Cain, through which he obtained the testimony that he was righteous, God testifying about his gifts, and through faith, though he is dead, he still speaks.

The author continues by citing examples and results of faith exhibited by people. He begins with Abel and says that his sacrifice was acceptable because it was offered in faith and, consequently, he was considered righteous (acceptable) by God. Abel's example of faith still speaks (his example continues to be mentioned throughout history and preserved in Scripture). The writer's point is that examples of faith are powerful witnesses that can extend beyond our lifetimes.

3. Enoch

> ⁵ By faith Enoch was taken up so that he should not see death; AND HE WAS NOT FOUND BECAUSE GOD TOOK HIM UP; for he obtained the witness that before his being taken up he was pleasing to God.

Enoch's faith was pleasing to God and, in some way, he was transported into the spiritual dimension without experiencing the conventional dying process. The key here is not the mysterious way he went to heaven but the fact that his faith was something that was pleasing to God. The author begins his examples from earliest history to show that faith was always what God looked for in men. Even His first act in natural history, creation, required faith in order to be observed with understanding.

Comment

> ⁶ And without faith it is impossible to please Him, for he who comes to God must believe that He is, and that He is a rewarder of those who seek Him.

The author now makes a second comment concerning faith which elaborates on his earlier statement. Not only does faith please God, it is impossible to please Him without it! God rewards those who have it (Enoch). It is the nature of faith to live in hope and to look towards things not seen, and in the next series of verses the author will mention people who demonstrated this vision based on faith. His point will be that people who have faith see something that other people do not.

4. Noah

> ⁷ By faith Noah, being warned by God about things not yet seen, in reverence prepared an ark for the salvation of his household, by which he condemned the world, and became an heir of the righteousness which is according to faith.

Noah believed God at His word about an unseen and highly unlikely event, and his faith responded in obedience (built the ark). His faith saved him and his household from the catastrophe. The writer adds that Noah preached to others for over a century but they disbelieved, and because of their disbelief (expressed in disobedience) were lost when the flood eventually came.

5. Abraham - Hebrews 11:8-12

The author reviews the life of one who truly saw a vision based on faith.

> [8] By faith Abraham, when he was called, obeyed by going out to a place which he was to receive for an inheritance; and he went out, not knowing where he was going. [9] By faith he lived as an alien in the land of promise, as in a foreign land, dwelling in tents with Isaac and Jacob, fellow heirs of the same promise; [10] for he was looking for the city which has foundations,

Abraham was called to move to an unknown land which God said would eventually be his. He wandered over it as a nomad all of his life never owning any part except the place where he buried his wife. Abraham lived in tents and yet, in faith, waited patiently for the special home promised to him by God.

> [11] By faith even Sarah herself received ability to conceive, even beyond the proper time of life, since she considered Him faithful who had promised; [12] therefore, also, there was born of one man, and him as good as dead at that, as many descendants AS THE STARS OF HEAVEN IN NUMBER, AND INNUMERABLE AS THE SAND WHICH IS BY THE SEASHORE.

Abraham was promised many descendants but his wife only bore him a single son long after child bearing years. Despite evidence to the contrary, Abraham never wavered in his belief that God would make good on His promise. In the middle of this discussion about Abraham's faith, the writer makes a third comment about those of which he has just spoken.

Comment — Hebrews 11:13-19

> [13] All these died in faith, without receiving the promises, but having seen them and having welcomed them from a distance, and having confessed that they were strangers and exiles on the earth. [14] For those who say such things make it clear that they are seeking a country of their own. [15] And indeed if they had been thinking of that country from which they went out, they would have had opportunity to return. [16] But as it is, they desire a better country, that is, a heavenly one. Therefore God is not ashamed to be called their God; for He has prepared a city for them.

All these died in faith without receiving the promises. However, having seen them and welcomed them from a distance, and having confessed that they were strangers and exiles on the earth, they made it clear that they were seeking a country of their own. Indeed, if they had been thinking of that country from which they went out, they would have had opportunity to return. But as it was, they desired a better country, a heavenly one! Therefore, God was not ashamed to be called their God for He had prepared a city just for them (the faithful).

The author explains that these people saw, by faith, the things that were promised (spiritual realities), but died before these promises were actually in hand (a better country/a homeland, are other ways of referring to heaven). However, because they saw these through faith, they were willing to bear the difficulties brought about by their vision, and never considered turning back to their original homeland, dying in the foreign lands where they wandered all of their lives.

These patriarchs did so because they believed, and because of this God was not ashamed to be associated with them

(God of Abraham, Isaac, Jacob - Exodus 3:15). The suggestion for the readers here is very clear: that returning to Judaism would be to abandon the vision. It would be a loss of faith which would cause them to be rejected by God. The idea that Christians are like "pilgrims" who are only passing through, on their way to a better place, is expressed here. Faithful people driven on by their vision of faith.

> [17] By faith Abraham, when he was tested, offered up Isaac; and he who had received the promises was offering up his only begotten son; [18] it was he to whom it was said, "IN ISAAC YOUR DESCENDANTS SHALL BE CALLED." [19] He considered that God is able to raise men even from the dead; from which he also received him back as a type.

The author refers back to Abraham one last time. He writes that Abraham responded to God's call and promise with belief. Now he will describe how Abraham responded with faith to God's test (asking him to sacrifice his only son). Abraham's faith was such that it obeyed God even beyond understanding. He was in the process of offering up the only son through whom God said his descendants would eventually come. Abraham believed (not that God would prevent him from sacrificing Isaac) that He could and would resurrect Isaac, if necessary, in order to fulfill His promise.

In effect, this is what happened: Isaac was as good as dead because Abraham was fully committed to sacrificing him. Abraham demonstrated the kind of faith that restores one from death so that all of his descendants now have an example of how faith overcomes everything, even death.

Final Parade

At this point, in shorter sequences, the author parades an entire series of Old Testament characters who faced a variety of trials in life but never wavered in their faith.

6. Isaac

> [20] By faith Isaac blessed Jacob and Esau, even regarding things to come.

Isaac blessed his sons, confident that God would carry out His purposes in them, despite their weaknesses and conflicts.

7. Jacob

> [21] By faith Jacob, as he was dying, blessed each of the sons of Joseph, and worshiped, leaning on the top of his staff.

Jacob passed on the blessing to his grandsons and refused to be buried in Egypt, giving instructions that his bones be returned to the land he was originally promised by God.

8. Joseph

> [22] By faith Joseph, when he was dying, made mention of the exodus of the sons of Israel, and gave orders concerning his bones.

Jacob's son, Joseph, made a similar request concerning his burial, which was carried out when the Israelites left Egypt (Exodus 13:19).

9. Moses

[23]By faith Moses, when he was born, was hidden for three months by his parents, because they saw he was a beautiful child; and they were not afraid of the king's edict. [24]By faith Moses, when he had grown up, refused to be called the son of Pharaoh's daughter; [25]choosing rather to endure ill-treatment with the people of God, than to enjoy the passing pleasures of sin; [26]considering the reproach of Christ greater riches that the treasures of Egypt; for he was looking to the reward. [27]By faith he left Egypt, not fearing the wrath of the king; for he endured, as seeing Him who is unseen. [28]By faith he kept the Passover and the sprinkling of the blood, so that he who destroyed the first-born might not touch them. [29]By faith they passed through the Red Sea as though they were passing through dry land; and the Egyptians, when they attempted it, were drowned.

In referring to Moses, the author shows how faith was present from the beginning to the end of his life:

- By faith he was hidden at birth.
- By faith he refused to deny his Jewish heritage.
- By faith he chose to be associated with his people, and suffered for it.
- By faith he led the people out of Egypt despite the danger.

- By faith he kept the Passover which ultimately saved the Jews from the Angel of Death.
- By faith he led his people across the Red Sea.

All these high points are recalled to show that Moses was a man of faith, and that faith enabled him to see God's promises. This vision also enabled him to respond to all of these challenges with courage.

10. Joshua

> [30] By faith the walls of Jericho fell down, after they had been encircled for seven days.

His name isn't mentioned, but Joshua's great faith is alluded to in this incident.

11. Rahab

> [31] By faith Rahab the harlot did not perish along with those who were disobedient, after she had welcomed the spies in peace.

She was the prostitute who risked her life in order to hide the Jewish spies. Again, courage prompted by the vision of faith.

12. Miscellaneous

> [32] And what more shall I say? for time will fail me if I tell of Gideon, Barak, Samson, Jephthah, of David

and Samuel and the prophets, [33]who by faith conquered kingdoms, performed acts of righteousness, obtained promises, shut the mouths of lions, [34]quenched the power of fire, escaped the edge of the sword, from weakness were made strong, became mighty in war, put foreign armies to flight. [35]Women received back their dead by resurrection; and others were tortured, not accepting their release, in order that they might obtain a better resurrection; [36]and others experienced mockings and scourgings, yes, also chains and imprisonment. [37]They were stoned, they were sawn in two, they were tempted, they were put to death with the sword; they went about in sheepskins, in goatskins, being destitute, afflicted, ill-treated [38](men of whom the world was not worthy), wandering in deserts and mountains and caves and holes in the ground.

At this point the author speeds up his procession, giving highlights of stories that he is sure his readers are familiar with. He has no time or space to list all of the things that faith produces in men and women: courage, deliverance from death, victory, ability to persevere in severe trial, as well as rejection and scorn from the world.

Comment

[39]And all these, having gained approval through their faith, did not receive what was promised, [40]because God had provided something better for us, so that apart from us they should not be made perfect.

In his final comment the author expands on his previous point concerning the common faith of all these people. The main idea is that these people lived, suffered and died never losing faith, but they did not receive the promises (freedom, forgiveness, true relationship with God, eternal life). This was not because God was cruel in denying them the reward.

The author explains that God did not want these people to receive the blessings before we, in the Christian era, did. It was not that Christians would have an easier time in practicing their faith, it was that they would see and possess the fulfillment of the promises that the people in the Old Testament only saw from afar.

Summary

- Faith has always been what God sought in men from the very beginning; it has always been what pleased Him.

- Faith was the basis upon which men could see spiritual realities and have the ability to obey God despite the difficulties caused by sin.

- The history of the Jewish nation is a history of faithful men and women in action.

- In the Old Testament people died without receiving the promises, but through faith saw them from afar.

- In the New Testament those promises are here and received by faith in Jesus Christ.

We need to understand that God requires the same thing from Christians today as He did from the Jews thousands of years ago: faith.

- Without faith we cannot please Him.
- Without faith we cannot see the promises.

- Without faith we will not have the ability to resist temptation and overcome the trials that each one of us will have to face in order to faithfully finish our lives as Christians.

You may be going along now without much thought to your faith, thinking all is well, but when your day of trial comes - then your faith will be examined. I hope it will be strong at that time.

CHAPTER 13
THE CHURCH OF CHRIST IS HOLY
- PART 1

Hebrews 12

I have shown that the author's purpose in this letter has been to persuade his readers not to abandon Christianity for Judaism. He does this by demonstrating how Jesus is more glorious than any part or personality within the Jewish religion. He then goes on to say that God's people, in every age, glorify Him by being faithful. His conclusion, therefore, is that Jesus' disciples should glorify Him by their faithfulness.

He illustrates this point by parading a long list of Jewish heroes who all persevered under trial but died without possessing the promise. The writer explains that by faith they saw these promises from afar, and died without giving up hope. The unmentioned point is that his readers have seen the promise of salvation realized in Jesus Christ and have a better basis for belief, as well as a stronger reason for hope, and thus should not abandon their faith. In fact, he says, they should persevere all the more!

Just as the vision of faith enabled the people of the Old Testament to overcome obstacles and die faithfully serving God, the much clearer vision, created by faith in the fully revealed plan of God through Christ, should motivate the people of the New Testament to holy living and service as well. In the final section of this epistle the author will describe the life made possible by one whose eyes are opened by faith in Jesus Christ.

The Example of Jesus — Hebrews 12:1-3

The people of the Old Testament saw the promises from afar and provided a good example of faithfulness under trial. Today, they see Jesus, and the author says that aside from the witness of faithfulness from past heroes, the Lord's example of faith under extreme conditions should be the motivating factor to holiness and perseverance for them.

> [1]Therefore, since we have so great a cloud of witnesses surrounding us, let us also lay aside every encumbrance, and the sin which so easily entangles us, and let us run with endurance the race that is set before us,

The author creates a scene where he compares the Christian life to a race where those who have successfully run in the past are now spectators cheering on the present contestants (Old Testament examples are the witnesses that surround the Christian in his race of faith). He adds that in the same way that long distance runners are lightly dressed and well trained, Christians must not be bogged down with sin and worldly concerns, and ready to run a race of endurance if they expect to finish.

> [2]fixing our eyes on Jesus, the author and perfecter of faith, who for the joy set before Him endured the cross, despising the shame, and has sat down at the right hand of the throne of God.

In the Old Testament they saw the promise of salvation from afar. Christians, however, clearly see salvation in Jesus Christ and are urged to fix their focus on Him, and not be distracted by any other thing. The reason for this is that our faith was not only initiated by Jesus (His words and deeds), it will be completed by Him since He is there to help us finish faithfully. He gives Jesus as the supreme example of a runner who has succeeded by reminding his readers that Jesus focused on the joy that He was to experience (sitting with God after obtaining our salvation). This focus enabled Him to endure the mocking, shame, suffering and death on the cross without losing faith or focus.

> [3]For consider Him who has endured such hostility by sinners against Himself, so that you may not grow weary and lose heart.

In every circumstance of the Christian's life, the key to finishing the race is to keep the focus on Jesus Christ and how He endured without failing to reach the end of His own race. Christian experience reminds us of the things we need to do to maintain that focus: a habit of daily prayer, regular worship and an ongoing study of His Word accompanied by a lifestyle devoted to obedience, service and Christian witness. These things guarantee that our focus on the prize of heaven will not waver. Concentrating on these matters will not tire us out or discourage us. It is sin, lack of focus on these things, and the inordinate love of the world that cause fatigue, discouragement, weakness and, ultimately, failure to finish the race.

Discipline, Proof of Sonship — 12:4-12

The author now addresses the difficulties that they are encountering as a result of their faith, and puts these into perspective. He tells them that these are not mindless events without purpose, but rather things that God uses to mold their character and perpetuate their faith.

> [4] You have not yet resisted to the point of shedding blood in your striving against sin;

After describing the faithful lives of the Old Testament personages and the supreme example of Christ, he asks them to compare their present suffering with that of those who came before them. If these saints did not give up the faith in the face of death, why should they do so now, especially since they were experiencing lesser challenges?

> [5] and you have forgotten the exhortation which is addressed to you as son,
> "MY SON, DO NOT REGARD LIGHTLY THE DISCIPLINE OF THE LORD,
> NOR FAINT WHEN YOU ARE REPROVED BY HIM;
> [6]FOR THOSE WHO THE LORD LOVES HE DISCIPLINES,
> AND HE SCOURGES EVERY SON WHOM HE RECEIVES."

He explains that trials and sufferings are used by God as a method to mold and teach them. Suffering is common to all men, but the fact that there are trials caused by faith is proof that some men are sons of God. Not all suffering is proof that we are children of God, lest this somehow become a criteria for salvation. However, suffering on account of faith is proof that God is working in one's life and the author says (by quoting the Old Testament - Deuteronomy 8:5; Proverbs 3:11-12) that this has always been so. For the one who disbelieves, his suffering produces little result and in the end becomes a sad reminder of sin and death. For the Christian, all suffering (specifically brought on by one's faith or as a result of human frailty) can and is used by God to produce spiritual maturity.

> [7] It is for discipline that you endure; God deals with you as with sons; for what son is there whom his father does not discipline? [8] But if you are without discipline, of which all have become partakers, then you are illegitimate children and not sons. [9] Furthermore, we had earthly fathers to discipline us, and we respected them; shall we not much rather be subject to the Father of spirits, and live?

Suffering for our faith's sake is a proof of sonship, and the author parallels a natural father's relationship to his son with God's relationship with Christians. At that time, illegitimate children were not considered worthy of their father's attention so an absence of trials (discipline) was a sign of inattention and illegitimacy. We expect fathers to discipline their children and so shouldn't be surprised that our heavenly Father disciplines His children as well. The author concludes that if we respect our earthly fathers and submit to their discipline, should we not respect or submit to our heavenly Father with a hope of greater results stemming from His correction?

> [10] For they disciplined us for a short time as seemed

> best to them, but He disciplines us for our good, that we may share His holiness. [11]All discipline for the moment seems not to be joyful, but sorrowful; yet to those who have been trained by it, afterwards it yields the peaceful fruit of righteousness.

The author continues his comparison of the discipline of earthly and heavenly fathers. He says that earthly parents are sinful, inconsistent, temporal and preparing us for life here on earth. In comparison, our heavenly Father is perfect, fair, can provide correction from the beginning to the end of our lives, and does so to make us holy like He is thus enabling us to share in His eternal nature.

The author concludes that discipline, both earthly and heavenly, is never pleasant but it is fruitful, especially when given by God because it ultimately produces the spiritual fruit of peace that comes from a right standing with Him. If we endure trials faithfully, our hope for eternal life will be very strong and this hope will produce peace of mind. After explaining the reasons for their suffering and possible benefits produced from this, the author goes on to encourage them.

Encouragement – 12:12-13

He has already mentioned the immature, weak, unfaithful and discouraged ones among them. Now he tells them to build up these brethren, and uses the illustration of a healthy body with weak and injured members to make his point. This exhortation has two steps:

> [12] Therefore, strengthen the hands that are weak and the knees that are feeble,

Brace up the weak member. This is done by encouragement, teaching, correction and help, not by anger or speaking against them.

> ¹³ and make straight paths for your feet, so that the limb which is lame may not be put out of joint, but rather be healed.

Go straight! Once the weak member is braced up, the rest of the body should go straight. In other words, once the spirit is supported it can more easily avoid the damaging effects of habitual sin. By bracing up the weak member and then going straight for the goal (spoken of before), the weak will be carried along by the strong and ultimately healed. In the church we do not amputate unless the member is dead. If the member is weak, we brace him up and carry him along.

Warning — 12:14-17

The writer goes from practical advice on what they should do, to a warning against the things they should avoid doing, and uses the example of Esau to make his point.

1. Avoid conflict

> ^{14A} Pursue peace with all men

It seems that the problems within this church were either caused by or were producing conflict. In addressing this he urges them to avoid conflict by pursuing peace. Conflict, even for the best of reasons, often causes many to turn from Christ. He tells them to find ways that produce peace. These methods are difficult because they usually challenge our sense of pride and coveted positions. Pursuing peace always costs something and usually the one who pays the greatest price is the one who is trying to produce the peace (i.e. Jesus gave up His innocent life in order to produce peace between God and sinful man).

2. Avoid unholy living

> [14b] and the sanctification without which no one will see the Lord.

To sanctify means to be separate unto the Lord. Avoid unholy alliances, unholy practices, unholy attitudes and pursue a continued separation of self to the Lord. Sanctified people encourage others, maintain peace within the assembly and should never be the cause for others to fall away.

3. Avoid spoiling others

> [15] See to it that no one comes short of the grace of God; that no root of bitterness springing up causes trouble, and by it many be defiled;

Some may give up following Christ because of many reasons (sin, faithlessness, cowardliness). Others act as a general cancer in that they fall away and, like a poison, bring others with them (their discouragement discourages others, their lack of faith weakens the faith of others, their sins infect and affect other people as well).

He warns these people that the damage that they cause to others may be irreparable even if they themselves one day repent.

> [16] that there be no immoral or godless person like Esau, who sold his own birthright for a single meal. [17]For you know that even afterwards, when he desired to inherit the blessing, he was rejected, for he found no place for repentance, though he sought for it with tears.

Some things we do cause destruction that cannot be repaired, even if we ourselves repent and change our ways. The author uses Esau as an example of one who exchanged his birthright as "first born" (and the blessings and privileges that accompanied this position) to his brother Jacob for a bowl of stew because he was hungry. Esau was an impulsive and unholy man, and this attitude caused him to make this foolish decision. Later on he regretted it, changed his mind and wept before God asking the Lord to give back his position, but it was too late.

We see that later on in his life Esau changed. He became wiser and more reverent of God. He reconciled with his brother, Jacob, but this didn't change the results of his previous mistakes. Those who spoil others may regret and repent, but many times the damage done cannot be undone.

Exhortation — 12:18-29

Originally, the author was giving practical instructions on what to do (encourage) and what to avoid doing (conflict, unholiness, spoiling others). In this passage he says that the reason why these practical instructions should be followed is because we belong to the kingdom of God and bad conduct will not go unpunished. This has always been and will continue to be so.

Comparing the settings of the old and the new

1. Judaism

> [18] For you have not come to a mountain that may be touched and to a blazing fire, and to darkness and gloom and whirlwind, [19]and to the blast of a trumpet and the sound of words which sound was such that those who heard begged that no further word should be spoken to them. [20]For they could not bear the command, "IF EVEAN A BEAST TOUCHES THE MOUNTAIN, IT WILL BE STONE." [21]And so terrible was the sight, that Moses said, "I AM FULL OF FEAR and trembling."

The author describes how the people of the Old Testament envisioned God and how God dealt with them. The scene he describes is from the people gathered at Mount Sinai in the desert (Exodus 19). Moses and the Israelites were terrified at the signs that heralded the presence of God among His people. These included a blazing fire, a trumpet blast, darkness and gloom, harsh words and a whirlwind that produced an awesome sight. Their image of God and His kingdom told them that they were not to come near for fear of defilement and death, that they were unworthy and unholy. Their fear urged them to obedience and yet, with all of this, they never were faithful to God. In other words, this terrifying vision never brought them any closer to living a holy and faithful life.

2. Christianity

> [22] But you have come to Mount Zion and to the city of the living God, the heavenly Jerusalem, and to myriads of angels, [23]to the general assembly and church of the first-born who are enrolled in heaven, and to God, the Judge of all, and to the spirits of righteous men made perfect, [24]and to Jesus, the mediator of a new covenant, and to the sprinkled blood, which speaks better than the blood of Abel.

The image of God revealed through the new covenant (Christianity) is one of God being with His people in heaven, not on earth. The scene is still awesome, majestic and glorious, but is not meant to instill fear or rejection, but rather one of praise, comfort and invitation. Christians are not gathered in the desert at Mount Sinai but at Mount Zion (old name for Jerusalem).

In the Old Testament, Jerusalem was the "City of God" because the temple was there. In the New Testament, "Jerusalem" was the symbol for heaven because that is where God actually dwelled. Christians are not surrounded by gloom, fire, whirlwind, a terrible sound of trumpets and harsh words. They are among myriads of angels (praising God), the church (brethren), God (Father), Jesus Christ (Lord and Savior) and His sacrifice which, unlike Abel's blood that cries out for vengeance, has another purpose. Jesus' blood permits forgiveness and opens the doors of this celestial city where Christians have been invited to enter in as eternal guests.

In arguing for proper conduct, the author first begins by comparing the two settings where the people found themselves - one in the past and the one they are now in. In the last verses of this chapter he will show that even though the settings are different, God is the same. He did not tolerate disobedience and unfaithfulness in the past and He doesn't tolerate it now or in the future either.

Obedience to God is Necessary — 12:25-27

> ²⁵ See to it that you do not refuse Him who is speaking. For if those did not escape when they refused him who warned them on earth, much less shall we escape who turn away from Him who warns from heaven.

He makes an argument that says: if they refused to heed God's warning given through the terrible signs of His presence here on earth, and were punished for it - imagine the culpability for those who have seen the signs of God's presence in the heavenly sanctuary - and still disobeyed! Christ who died, resurrected and ascended into heaven is He who speaks and He who warns (from heaven) to remain faithful and to obey.

> ²⁶ And His voice shook the earth then, but now He has promised, saying, "YET ONCE MORE I WILL SHAKE NOT ONLY THE EARTH, BUT ALSO THE HEAVEN." ²⁷And this expression, "Yet once more," denotes the removing of those things which can be shaken, as of created things, in order that those things which cannot be shaken may remain.

When God's voice spoke the first time (gave the Law, established His people and His holy place), the entire world shook and was affected. Verse 26 is taken from Haggai 2:6 (Old Testament prophet) who wrote about the reconstruction of the temple during the period of restoration. His thought was that once the temple was built, God would shake the nations in order to fill it with all of their treasures. The author of Hebrews takes this passage and uses it in connection with the end of the world stating that when Jesus returns, not only will the nations be shaken but the entire cosmic order will be dissolved (II Peter 3:10). The point here is that when this happens, only those things that cannot be destroyed will survive and the only thing that will survive the return of Jesus will be His faithful and obedient church (those who encourage and avoid conflict, unholy living and spoiling others) all else will be destroyed.

Summary

The author begins the chapter by explaining to his readers that the clearer view that they have of God through Jesus and His promises should produce a stronger faith in them than in the past. He says that this faith should motivate them to holiness and perseverance, despite the obstacles they face. He reminds them that when they encounter trials they should:

- Stay focused on Christ, not the trials, the world or themselves.

- Remember that trials are a proof of legitimate sonship where God is perfecting their faith.

- Realize that trials are not a punishment. They are a spiritual refining process if endured with faith.

He continues by telling them to encourage each other, especially the weak, and avoid things like conflict and unholy living which discourage others and destroy faith.

Finally, in verses 28-29 he tells them to be grateful for the blessings that they have in Christ.

[28] Therefore, since we receive a kingdom which cannot be shaken, let us show gratitude, by which we may offer to God an acceptable service with reverence and awe; [29]for our God is a consuming fire.

He shows how blessed they are by comparing the revelation of God that the Old Testament people had compared to the glorious one given to them in the New Testament. The comparison suggests that to reject God's offer of grace revealed through Christ is the height of ingratitude since it is revealed so gloriously and promises so much. The chapter ends with the reminder that the glory of God and His mercy revealed by Christ does not erase the terrifying side of His justice which will be exercised on all who reject His offer of mercy and forgiveness.

Our trials and difficulties overwhelm us only when we remove our focus from Jesus and begin concentrating exclusively on our problems. We become unfaithful and see no difference in our lives but foolishly ignore the fact that we could be swept away in a moment without Christ. The prayer, study and strengthening of our faith through service and worship prepare us for the day when the storm comes. And when it does come, we need to remember more than ever that we must keep our eyes on the Lord, not the storm.

Trials and suffering are part of everyone's lives, believer and non-believer alike. Being a Christian does not protect us from suffering. In fact, in many cases it causes more problems. We need to remember that even though we may suffer various trials, this is not a sign that God is punishing us. On the contrary, it is usually a reminder that God is intimately involved in our lives. Unlike unbelievers, our trials can work to produce everlasting rewards. Therefore, let us never use our trials as an excuse to abandon Christ or the church. We should try to see these things as tools that God uses to test our faith and create in us a more Christ-like character.

It is important to have a proper vision of God. Unfortunately, as sinful human beings, we tend to see God as we want to see Him (nice God, funny God, indulgent God, mean God), but the only description of God that has any accuracy is the one contained in His Word. It says that He is merciful, kind and compassionate to those who seek, obey and trust Him; but it also says that for those who disobey, who are unfaithful and ungrateful, that He is a consuming fire. A proper attitude in prayer, worship and conduct will only be developed when we recognize both facets of God's character: His love **and** His justice. This proper vision of Him will help us avoid the extremes of becoming too frightened of Him or too complacent about Him.

CHAPTER 14
THE CHURCH OF CHRIST IS HOLY
- PART 2

Hebrews 13

After showing how the Lord Jesus glorified His church through His ministry, death, resurrection and ascension to the right hand of God, the author goes on to encourage his readers to respond in kind by glorifying Jesus as His church. He tells them that they can do this by living holy lives and remaining faithful to Him, despite the many trials they face as Christians.

This holy lifestyle would be evident if they:

- Encouraged those among them who were weak spiritually to remain faithful.

- Avoided conflict, immorality and unseemly behavior that could cause a fellow Christian to lose faith.

- Were grateful for their secure position as those who would survive the destruction of the world at the return of Jesus.

The author ends his letter with the reminder that God always punished those who disobeyed Him, so they should be careful to heed this warning. The final verses list additional features that are found in a church that is holy.

Love the Brethren

> [1] Let love of the brethren continue. [2]Do not neglect to show hospitality to strangers, for by this some have entertained angels without knowing it. [3]Remember the prisoners, as though in prison with them, and those who are ill-treated, since you yourselves also are in the body.

This is not an appeal to begin loving one another but an encouragement that love should continue to be a common feature of their lifestyle. The Greek term (*xenos philios*) translated into the English word hospitality literally meant, "The love of strangers." In the first century Christian preachers and teachers travelled extensively spreading the gospel and teaching God's Word to congregations spread throughout the Roman Empire. Hosting these individuals was a very important part of the overall ministry of evangelism.

Aside from the assistance it provided to those who were planting and helping churches to grow at that time, the writer says that hospitality also afforded unforeseen benefits to those who provided it. His reference to "angels" is from Genesis 18:2 where Abraham unknowingly offered hospitality to the Lord Himself as he welcomed three strangers to his tent.

Hospitality is not simply having someone into your home, it is kindness to others who are not necessarily known to you. The author gives the example of prisoners (probably Christians who have been imprisoned for their faith). He says that his readers may not know these people and others who may also be suffering in some way, but as fellow Christians, can relate to them and perhaps even minister to them since they too are part of the body of Christ.

Sexual Purity

> [4] Let marriage be held in honor among all, and let the marriage bed be undefiled; for fornicators and adulterers God will judge.

This is a general exhortation to marital fidelity. God honors the intimacy enjoyed within marriage but will punish those who violate this and His other commands regarding proper sexual conduct.

Contentment

> [5] Let your character be free from the love of money, being content with what you have; for He Himself has said, "I WILL NEVER DESERT YOU, NOR WILL I EVER FORSAKE YOU," [6]so that we confidently say, "THE LORD IS MY HELPER, I WILL NOT BE AFRAID, WHAT SHALL MAN DO TO ME?" [7]Remember those who led you, who spoke the word of God to you; and considering the result of their conduct, imitate their faith.

Here the writer establishes the goal and attitude for Christians regarding wealth. He says that they should be free from the love of money, not from wealth itself, because the love of money leads one to judge most matters based on personal profit and the acquiring of things. People like this are always afraid that they will not have enough and if they don't acquire, they will be destitute. The author encourages them to seek contentment or satisfaction (filled up, unafraid) with what they already have whether great or small.

Satisfaction is not based on what we manage to acquire but on the assurance that God gives to His people. The promise is that He will never abandon His own and will always be there to help and defend His people. The writer says that their confidence should be based on God's promise to care for them, not on their ability to acquire money.

Warning Against Strange Doctrines — Hebrews 13:7-16

A holy church will faithfully keep the teachings of Christ. In this section he exhorts them to heed those who taught them in the past, next he refers to the various doctrinal issues they face at the moment, then he tells them to pay attention to their current teachers.

1. Remember those who brought you to faith.

> [7] Remember those who led you, who spoke the word of God to you; and considering the result of their conduct, imitate their faith.

They need to remember their original teachers and the teachings that brought them to Christ in the first place. These people were obviously gone now, but this church was encouraged to imitate their faithful lifestyle in order to finish as faithful disciples of Christ just as their teachers did before them.

2. Consider their teaching versus the false doctrine which is swirling around you now.

> [8] Jesus Christ is the same yesterday and today and forever.

He establishes that the first thing they were taught, the glory and supremacy of Christ, is as true now as it was then, and will always be true. Circumstances change, doctrines come and go, but Jesus always remains.

The author has reviewed how Jesus and His ministry were superior to every aspect of the Jewish religion. Now he makes one final argument showing how the Christian worship of God, offered by the disciples of Jesus, was superior to that offered by those people still trying to worship God through Judaism. One criticism of Christian worship by these people was that there was no sacrifice or no way for the individual to participate in the offering of something tangible to God. The author argues that Christians do have a sacrifice and a worship very much acceptable to God.

> [9a] Do not be carried away by varied and strange teachings;

He begins with a general warning not to be swept away by false teaching, and refers to the many incorrect teachings that centered on food. Some doctrines restricted certain foods, others held up consumption of food as worship. The general idea was that either the abstinence from or indulgence in food made you more or less acceptable to God. The author reminds them that food's purpose was to strengthen the body, not the heart (soul) of man. To strengthen the soul, one needed the grace of God, not food laws (Romans 14:17; I Corinthians 8:8).

> [9b] for it is good for the heart to be strengthened by grace, not by foods, through which those who were thus occupied were not benefited.

This verse is a bridge idea leading to his main thought. There were many who were overly concerned about food issues and it did not benefit them. He refers to the ones to whom food was very important, the Jews. The specific food he targets is the meat of the sacrifice offered and eaten by the priests. The Jews were saying that because Christian worship had no animal (meat) sacrifices, their worship had no real substance.

> [10] We have an altar, from which those who serve the tabernacle have no right to eat.

In response to this the author claims that Christians do have an altar/sacrifice (uses the word "altar" to represent the entire process of sacrificial offerings in Jewish worship). He explains further that Christians share a sacrifice that the Jewish priests have no right to share in! It is interesting to note that he refers to them as the servants of the tent (tabernacle) and not the servants of God since God is no longer in the earthly temple. His conclusion is that at this point the Jewish priests are only serving the building, not God

> [11] For the bodies of those animals whose blood is brought into the holy place by the high priest as an

offering for sin, are burned outside the camp.

This is a reference to the practice of the high priests who, on the Day of Atonement, would not eat any part of the sacrifice but would take it outside of the camp and totally destroy it by fire (it was to be wholly offered to God in this way). The ashes of the sacrifice would then be mixed with water and used in purification rites. The significance of having the animal completely destroyed and removed from the camp was that the sins which they bore were also removed from the camp as well.

[12] Therefore Jesus also, that He might sanctify the people through His own blood, suffered outside the gate.

Here, he parallels Jesus' sacrifice to this practice by saying that this ritual in the Old Testament typified the cross of Christ. He also suffered and died outside the camp/city (Calvary was outside the city of Jerusalem) and His blood/sacrifice also purified the people from sin.

[13] Hence, let us go out to Him outside the camp, bearing His reproach. [14]For here we do not have a lasting city, but we are seeking the city which is to come.

He continues to explain that just as the people went to the priests to be purified by the ashes of the sacrifice of atonement, they now should go to Jesus for purification. He is our sacrifice/altar and, because of their disbelief, He is the sacrifice that the priests had no right to share in. However, going to Jesus for purification meant two things:

1. A person had to go outside of the camp - away from Judaism.

2. A person had to be ready to bear the reproach for being counted with Jesus.

Going to Jesus, outside of the camp/city, might bring one a reproach, but the camp and sacrifice that the Jews were clinging to were not going to last anyways. Leaving the old city was the only way to find the new and eternal city of God.

> [15] Through Him then, let us continually offer up a sacrifice of praise to God, that is, the fruit of lips that give thanks to His name. [16]And do not neglect doing good and sharing; for with such sacrifices God is pleased.

Our author finishes by encouraging them to continue worshipping God with a worship that was indeed valid, not the empty ritual of Judaism but the very real exercise of Christian worship. This included praise to God with gratitude, the doing of good works and loving encouragement for all. These things, done in the name of Christ, was true worship and superior to what the Jews were involved in at the time when this letter was written.

Obey present leaders

> [17]Obey your leaders, and submit to them; for they keep watch over your souls, as those who will give an account. Let them do this with joy and not with grief, for this would be unprofitable for you.

He has encouraged them to remember former teachers, exposed the fallacy of some of the false teachings they faced, and now charges them to obey present leaders and teachers. The leaders they now had obviously maintained the same attitude and teachings that their original leaders had promoted. These were faithful men and he exhorts the church to obey them (follow their instructions) and submit to them (acknowledge their leadership).

He also tells them why this should be their attitude. A church leader's responsibility is to watch over souls. This task should not be made more difficult than it already is by a disobedient (to the Word) and rebellious (to the leadership) church. This type of response would not profit them because it would not promote church growth and would also bring the Lord's punishment on the guilty parties.

Closing Remarks — Hebrews 13:18-25

Letters in the Hellenistic (Greek) period followed a set pattern at the beginning and end. The final words of the author of Hebrews follow this style of writing:

- Prayer
- Final remarks
- Greetings from the author

1. Prayer

The author asks them to pray for him and he, in turn, offers a prayer for his readers.

Prayer request

> [18] Pray for us, for we are sure that we have a good conscience, desiring to conduct ourselves honorable

> in all things. [19]And I urge you all the more to do this, that I may be restored to you the sooner.

He asks that they pray that he be restored to them soon. His conscience is clear and he is sure that what he has written is correct. What he wants now is to be with them again in person.

Prayer on their behalf

> [20] Now the God of peace, who brought up from the dead the great Shepherd of the sheep through the blood of the eternal covenant, even Jesus our Lord, [21]equip you in every good thing to do His will, working in us that which is pleasing in His sight, through Jesus Christ, to whom be the glory forever and ever. Amen.

He prays that God will equip them with everything necessary to do His will (faith, knowledge, courage), and he is assured that they know that God's will is that through the spreading of the gospel, Jesus Christ and His church will be glorified.

2. Final remarks

> [22] But I urge you, brethren, bear with this word of exhortation, for I have written to you briefly. [23]Take notice that our brother Timothy has been released, with whom, if he comes soon, I shall see you.

The writer now makes the only two personal remarks contained in this letter. First, he refers to his letter as an exhortation and hopes they will receive it kindly, even though there are some pointed references in it. Secondly, he speaks of Timothy, the evangelist, and the hope he has of being reunited with him and them soon. He also refers to Timothy's imprisonment which is the only time this is mentioned in the New Testament.

3. Greeting

> [24] Greet all of your leaders and all the saints. Those from Italy greet you. [25]Grace be with you all.

He greets two separate groups: the leaders (elders and teachers) and the saints (others in the church). He also mentions other brothers in Italy and completes the letter with a typical Christian ending that confers a blessing on his readers.

Summary

This final section can be summarized by asking and answering one question:

How does a faithful and holy church glorify its Lord?

1. It encourages weak brethren to carry on faithfully.
2. It avoids conflict, immorality and bad examples.
3. It demonstrates love and hospitality among the brethren.
4. It practices sexual purity.
5. It relies on God, not money for security.

6. It does not follow strange teachings and teachers, but submits to its leaders who themselves submit to Christ and His Word.

7. It continually offers to God acceptable worship through prayers of thanksgiving and good works in Jesus' name.

I direct you to verse 8 in this last chapter as a final word of encouragement now that our study of this epistle is complete:

> Jesus Christ is the same yesterday
> and today and forever.

The author of Hebrews encouraged these brethren of long ago to be faithful to Jesus until the end.

In the same way, through my own teaching of this epistle, I also encourage you to remain faithful to the glorious Jesus because He was faithful to them yesterday, is faithful to us today and will be faithful forevermore. Praise be to His name!

ALSO AVAILABLE FROM
BIBLETALK BOOKS

BibleTalk.tv is an Internet Mission Work.

We provide textual Bible teaching material on our website and mobile apps for free. We enable churches and individuals all over the world to have access to high quality Bible materials for personal growth, group study or for teaching in their classes.

The goal of this mission work is to spread the gospel to the greatest number of people using the latest technology available. For the first time in history it is becoming possible to preach the gospel to the entire world at once. BibleTalk.tv is an effort to preach the gospel to all nations every day until Jesus returns.

The Choctaw Church of Christ in Oklahoma City is the sponsoring congregation for this work and provides the oversight for the BibleTalk ministry team. If you would like information on how you can support this ministry, please go to the link provided below.

bibletalk.tv/support

Printed in Great Britain
by Amazon